NOT ALL SNAKES

RATTLE

BREAKING THE IDENTITY OF ADDICTION

By
Samuel George

Acknowledgements

Dad- It is impossible for me to articulate the impact my father has had on my life. He died in July of 2024. It seems I continue to grieve his loss daily and the void still has tremendous weight. He always saw the best in me, and knew me better than I knew myself. My nickname for my dad was Yoda, because it always felt like I was listening to wisdom and someone who understood life like he had the manual to it. You always told me to write a book Dad because people needed to hear what I had to share. I'll do my best, you are always with me.

Taylor- My youngest of two sons and my connection to greatness. No matter my faults, you have loved me in the purest sense possible - unconditionally. Thank you for your unwavering support and for always being a wonderful human being. You have taught me far more than I've taught you son.

Metallica- Music plays a tremendous impact in my life and Metallica has at times, literally, kept me alive. Many of their songs express a connection to addiction that has granted me just enough emotional and spiritual reprieve to get me through a moment, and at times, a day. Simply put, they have played an important part in saving my life repeatedly just because I want to hear more.

Skip- To my older brother. You have always been my moral compass and you have taught me the value of integrity. From wiffle ball to sled rides when we were kids, you've made a tremendous impact on my life. You have been a wonderful example of being a father, and a man.

Nick- There is no way I would have made it to rehab without you. I'm proud and honored to call you my friend. Keep up the great work, you have a lot to offer the world.

Dallas Jenkins - The creator of The Chosen. Thank you for pursuing your God given talent of storytelling. The show reconnected me to Jesus and the courage to write this book. God gave me the name of this book, and the titles of the chapters, as I was watching The Chosen.

DEDICATION

I would like to dedicate this book to anyone who is struggling with addiction and its relentless grip. My compassion, sympathy, and empathy to all of us who identify with this illness, my heart goes out to you. Additionally, this book goes out to anyone who has lost someone to addiction not just through death, but to those who are estranged or relationships destroyed because it's too risky to emotionally invest. As I write this, I myself have two people I adore who aren't in my life because the damage I caused while in active addiction has created an understandable distance. Lastly, I want to dedicate this book to all those who have shown me there is a better way to live life. People in N/A, A/A, shows like The Chosen, pastors like Joby Martin, and Steven Furtick. God bless all those who believe and even those who don't, I was once unsure myself.

FOREWORD

The spiritual insight and wisdom that comes from this body of masterful work, is life changing. Samuel George's life's experience and wisdom he has gained from his path to recovery, to finding the Lord Jesus Christ as his personal savior, will take you on a transformational journey that is sure to impact your life forever. If you are one who desires to know God on a deeper level than just considering a religion, but rather a relationship, this book is for you. Especially if you are trying to overcome addiction. Each chapter helped me to understand the struggle of the addict on a deeper level. Every chapter increased my faith about life after death, and this book strengthened my faith as Sam made his case about the proof of Jesus's divinity. Got questions about recovery and faith...this book has the answers. It is a must read!!!

Dr. Vincent Henderson C.C.C. Certified Christian Counselor

Overseer/Founder at Freedom City Church and The Freedom Agency Counseling and Coaching, Ocala Florida

Table of content

Chapter 1 12
The God Hole 12
Chapter 2 21
Modern Day Profit (Prophet) 21
Chapter 3 28
JAGGED EDGE 28
Chapter 4 36
ADDITION BY SUBTRACTION 36
Chapter 5 45
THE GOOD SHEPHERD 45
Chapter 6 56
BEING A CONDUIT 56
Chapter 7 66
THE THORN IN MY SIDE 66
Chapter 8 76
DAILY REPRIEVE 76
Chapter 9 85
THE VOICE OF GOD 85
Chapter 10 92
PROOF OF GOD 92
Came To Believe (Part 1) 92
Chapter 11 98
THE BIBLE 98
CAME TO BELIEVE (PART 2) 98
Chapter 12 106
The Resurrection 106
Came To Believe (Part 3) 106
Chapter 13 117
DO YOU WANT TO BE HEALED? 117

CONCLUSION 122

INTRODUCTION

I died three times in 2023 from drug overdoses. I'm writing this book to save my life and equally as important, perhaps your life. As I begin to put pen to paper, it occurs to me there may be no flow and certainly no professional writer's precision of connecting thoughts in a manner that shows I've perfected my craft.

What I do have is my story, complete transparency, and I will tell you this is an assignment from God. This isn't some "burning bush" moment, but for the first time in my life, the God of my understanding is giving me what I've always wanted, direct communication. It is my hope that what follows will connect with just one person and in so doing change the trajectory of a life- including my own.

I will do my best to convey my story, my daily struggle, and to let you know that if no one has told you lately, you matter. At the very least I understand what it is to think, feel, process life, fail, succeed, and everything in between as an addict. By no means do I have addiction "solved" and throughout this book will be references to 12 step influences, the Bible, and God, as being tools in the toolbox to navigate through the insidious nature of addiction.

I'm writing this to save my life and if you're reading this, so are you. Perhaps you have a loved one who is addicted or have lost someone to addiction. My hope is this book will provide healing and as a result we can attempt to get on with our lives. I'm only here as a result of God's grace and the power of Jesus Christ. I was the biggest cynic as it pertained to the God of the Bible that I knew. It wasn't that I didn't believe in God, but the exclusivity that Christianity claimed struck me as arrogant. Please don't let the fact that I'm convinced Christianity is for me, make you put this book down. Ask God to reveal himself to you, and I believe he will.

I feel I have found many answers, yet I fail at executing them and rigorous honesty is all I seek to connect with throughout this book. I have no idea where this book will lead and I'm horrified to write it and horrified not to write it.

I have been an addict for over 30 years
Some of the content will be graphic including language, sexual content, and at times the use of drugs will be explained only as needed.

Chapter 1

The God Hole

The truth of the matter is, if I could successfully use drugs, there's a greater likelihood than not I'd keep using. It's a little embarrassing to admit I like the way drugs make me feel, and how they make me not feel. The complete spontaneity of who I might meet and what environment any given day or night may hold. There's a sense of belonging when I got high around others, and also the occasions of feeling complete freedom isolating at times would provide. There were times when I was the one with the money and therefore a certain level of accommodation was provided. Whether it was something as simple as someone giving up their seats so I could break everyone off, or different women "wanting to hang out." All of it provided a dysfunctional form of connection and status. When I showed up, it meant money for the dealers, laughter in the air, and a feeding of the beast all addicts crave and chase. I'd watch others' personalities change when I showed up, including mine. I was the guy everyone wanted to be with and I had no shortage of "friends".

At this point in my life I was roughly 18 months removed from doing 12 years in prison. I'll explain all that later, but I had rebuilt my life as a result of becoming a certified dog trainer while in prison. Typically, once a month or so, I would travel about an hour away from where I lived and party my ass off. On average it was $1000-$1500 I'd spend over a day or two, and this particular MO went on for nearly 2 years.

My history and drug use at this point of my life had been extensive. There isn't a drug I haven't tried but personally cocaine has always been my preference. Crack specifically, but at times I can still feel the needle in my arm and taste the wave of a shot from mainlining. Like many of us, I started around 15 with pot and it just slowly was like a hole in me was filled as I continued my experimenting. That's the only way I can explain it - a hole. A hole that was never filled, never satisfied, never content, because as an addict the truth of the matter is, we always just want more. Anything that makes us feel better we want more of it. Gambling, food, drugs, sex, money, power, influence, clothes, binge-watching - feel free to add to the list.

This disease will eat you from the inside out like cancer and doesn't give a damn about who or what is in its wake. Addiction is a silent killer that slowly erodes all aspects of our nature: mind, body, spirit, emotion. It even wants us to get well so that it can take it away. Stealthy, cunning, waiting, waiting, waiting... like a snake without a rattle. Waiting for us to get our lives back in order, families restored, just so it can take it all over again. Although truth be told, we actually give it away, consumed whole by our own self destruction.

I could write countless chapters on the topic and give hundreds of war stories. However, any addict reading this book doesn't need to be educated or informed on drugs or alcohol, what they do, how they destroy our lives or those closest to us. To those who might read this because of a loved one; the loneliness, helplessness, and complete despair you must feel I cannot fathom. I don't know what it's like to be on the other side of loving an addict, it's always been a one-way street for me as the addict.

Just so everyone is aware, currently, I am in rehab. So what I feel I have is the gift of desperation and absolutely nothing to lose including my life. I can tell you I'm not afraid of dying, I'm afraid of living. The constant daily battle of feeling like there is something inside me that wants me dead, the addiction.

I also want to be transparent that I am diagnosed with bipolar disorder, PTSD, OCD, and general anxiety disorder. I have chosen not to be medicated although yes I have tried medications. I can't stand the way they make me feel sluggish, like I'm in mental quicksand. To each their own on this topic, I'm just sharing my position. Those pills are attempting to fill a "hole" I believe only the spiritual realm can overcome and subsequently fill. It's interesting to me that if you replace the letter 'c' in medication to a 't' the word becomes meditation. Medication is from the outside in, meditation is from the inside out. This is by no means a practice I've perfected, but I can attest to the fact it helps me more than any medication.

As far as character defects are concerned, when I was in active addiction I had them all. Lying, blaming, manipulating, overreacting, creating drama, gas lighting, yelling, making unreasonable demands, playing the victim, shallow apologies - you get the point. Countless relapses after I promised myself and to those I loved it would never happen again, yet it did. The ensuing guilt and shame that the predatory self-defeating thought processes we all harbor as a result of being addicts, becomes fertile ground to keep us feeling like there is no way out.

As far as my children are concerned, I have two sons, currently 33, and 23. My oldest and I haven't spoken now in almost 18 years. Out of respect for the choice to not have me in his life, he will remain anonymous. What I will share is I was a single father at age 19 and had custody of him until he was 16. Continuous relapses and watching me slowly essentially committing suicide, he was forced to save himself from my lack of taking responsibility for the disease. He spent the last two years in high school being taken care of by my brother, mom and sister. The "hole" I've been conveying to you, just got deeper.

My younger son Taylor has a different mom than my older son, and I was married to Taylor's mom. From ages 6-16, Taylor didn't have me in his life, I was in prison. The "hole" just got deeper. There was very little contact during that time although I wrote as many letters as I could, and my dad did his best as well to maintain communication with his grandson. I'll discuss more on this time later, but as of now Taylor and I have never been closer and despite my behavior he has always believed in me, been loyal, and the best son a dad could ever hope for.

A brief synopsis of my work history: I was manager of Taco Bell for 9 years, ran a delivery route for Boar's Head, worked in the corporate world at Raymond James Financial and was working there when they gained the naming rights for the stadium the Tampa Bay Buccaneers currently play in. I've worked at a window tint distribution warehouse, and then a lead trainer at a medical service dog organization as well as my own dog training LLC with my significant other at the time - the other person who will remain anonymous.

I bring this up to let you know since the late '90s, my last four jobs all ended as a result of drugs- the "hole" just got deeper. What is also vital, in fact necessary for us to relate, is I'm going to ask for you to look for any similarities not differences in what I'm sharing. This disease will attempt to pick you out like a wounded gazelle from the herd. I've explained it's predatory in nature, I'm doing the best to show you how. If you catch yourself assassinating my character or taking my inventory, this is the disease attempting to mentally isolate you and convince you that you're different. I say this to talk with you not at you because someone has had to point these signals out to me. Addiction is like a toxic poison in our thought processes, like a snake waiting, no rattle.

Just know that moving forward there isn't any character defect, attitude, belief system or dialogue that I've not had myself on the topic of addiction. There have been countless hours of reading on the topic in a variety of categories: religion, spiritual, biological, psychological, physiological, anything that could help me figure out addiction. I have a PHD in absolutely nothing but burning my life to the ground. Countless attempts and simply implementing will power to stop always seem to fail.

One attitude and subconscious belief system I've come to see in myself, seems to be a common denominator in a lot of addicts. Here is a chance to look for our similarities not differences. I have been a person who either finds a solution to every problem or finds a problem with every solution. As for me specifically, I tend to think in black and white, not gray. It's box A or box B. My addictive thought processes at times use this against me to get well and stay well. I tend to want to know a projected definitive result before I make decisions and act. Oftentimes, it has kept me in a state of indecisiveness which in turn, leads to no decision. Not making a decision is actually making a decision as whatever situation will default into a result because I've not been proactive in guiding my own life.

My thoughts are inescapably in one of three places 1. Past 2. Present 3. Future. Because I've never felt connected to any long term purpose, I constantly mismanage the present. For example, no matter how much money I have, I spend it. When I'm in active addiction it's all going to go towards the cause of feeding the beast. It's a bottomless pit, a hole, that I can only describe as feeling like I'm starving and can't get enough to eat.

As the addiction spider webs out into all tentacles of our being, it occupies that hole and lives there.

Active addiction brings out the worst in human characteristics and attributes. It reminds me of the "7 deadly sins"- pride, anger, greed, lust, envy, gluttony, sloth. I could spend the rest of the book diving into any and all of these defects of character. However, it is said there are universal laws that govern the world in which we live, and you've probably always heard something like everything has an opposite - up/down, left/right, good/bad etc... So here's the first piece of good news I can present. If the 7 deadly sins represent our defects, it stands to reason we have the assets. Addiction doesn't want you to know that. Even knowing this to be true, I continue to fail at implementing and cultivating assets in my life.

My life has been like the portrayal of the movie Titanic. Despite knowing the outcome, I will convince myself I'll turn the ship in time and never hit the iceberg. I'm hypnotized by the movie every time it's on and it perfectly mimics the insanity of how addiction looks in my life. Despite knowing the outcome, I always root for the damn ship to turn and every time it hits the iceberg. I've seen this movie before and it always ends the same! My life gets destroyed over and over despite having all the information needed to make a different decision. It is my romanticized illusion that I will someday, somehow, be able to successfully use drugs and have a fulfilling life. Yet, I continue to do the very thing that is killing me- WHY?

        Romans 7: 15-20

I do not understand my own actions. For I do not do what I want, but I do the very thing I hate. But I know that nothing good dwells in me, that is, in my flesh. I can will what is right, but I cannot do it. For I do not do the good I want, but the evil I do not want is what I do.

This was written by Paul in the New Testament nearly 2000 years ago. Addiction wasn't as prevalent or perhaps recognized then, but what strikes me as human beings is we have been sharing the same experience. There is something at our core that undeniably wants what we know is bad for us. Left to my own devices, I repeatedly appear hardwired to self-destruct.

I'd like to reference the first step in any 12-step program: "we admitted we were powerless over our addiction and our lives had become unmanageable." I have found the 12 steps to be a tool in my toolbox to help me. Let me translate what the first step says to me - we're screwed! My best thinking has got me right where I am in life. Clearly, me, myself, and I, suck at implementing enough willpower to beat the disease of addiction.

Let me address the disease part now because of years of my own experience and debates with people who say they just quit cold turkey and therefore we all should too. I'm glad that worked for you, but don't you dare paint us all with one broad stroke. The American Medical Association classified alcoholism as a disease in 1956 and included addiction as a disease in 1987. As a result, it consists of three components: 1. Chronic 2. Progressive 3. Fatal. Let me quote the big book of alcoholics anonymous "The fact is that most alcoholics and addicts have lost the power of choice. Our so-called willpower becomes practically non-existent. We are unable at certain times to bring into our consciousness with sufficient force the memory of the suffering and humiliation of even a week or a month ago. We are without defense against the first drink."

The book Dopamine Nation by Dr. Anna Lembke, discusses this on a biological and physiological level. There are grooves in our neural pathways like little ditches equivalent to a built-in infrastructure in our brain. These grooves represent and channel our learned behavioral processes. Default settings of what our brain, essentially a super computer, defaults to. It's like brain muscle memory. Let me note here that I'm giving you my interpretations as just a common person trying to save my life and I'm sharing with you what I feel I've learned along the way. It appears our thoughts can now measurably and quantifiably be observed on a biological and physiological level so "as a man thinketh so is he" has never been more true.

My mind thinks it has to know, how it knows, what it knows, before it will accept it. Where are we to find the strength, awareness, and most importantly power to fight this entity that we continue to battle? The answer reminds me of a story I read about the late escape artist Harry Houdini. Houdini was placed in a straight jacket, handcuffed, and then put in a jail cell with a big padlock on the cell door. Houdini managed to get out of the cuffs, out of the straight jacket, but could not solve the riddle of the lock - his escape attempt failed. He then calls the jailer over and questions him about the lock. The jailer said " Harry, I assure you it's an ordinary lock. I thought you'd figure it out quickly, so I never bothered locking it. All you had to do was push open the door, and walk out." This story summarizes what I feel has been my experience and I suppose yours as well. I thought I could outsmart and out-think addiction much like Houdini thought he had to solve the riddle of the lock.

Much of what I've learned about addiction is it's a disease of the mind. Einstein said "you cannot solve a problem with the same mindset that created it." The answer to addiction isn't mental, although our brain physiologically will influence it.

This is where I will begin to search for God or be open to the possibility of a creator.

Step 2 "came to believe that a power greater than ourselves could restore us to sanity." I will do my best to convey a message that has been sought by man from our beginning of time. Does God exist? How do I know? What happens after death? I want to relay that my parents died 6 weeks apart in the summer of 2024. I feel I've been catapulted into unchartered waters as I quickly am forced to deal with my own mortality. Both my parents were 84, went through loving me through my addiction, and died knowing I was at least trying to overcome my addiction. As I have concentrated on writing this book, there have been days I am consumed by darkness, depression, and an internal narrative that it's useless to do it. Do I seriously think by sharing my journey through an addicted life will help me or anyone else? Negative thoughts come like arrows across my consciousness and yet something inside me, perhaps just the will to live, pushes me to just keep writing, just keep trying.

Chapter 2

Modern Day Profit (Prophet)

In my mid-20s, I was hired at Raymond James Financial and worked exclusively with the NASDAQ stock market. I'll never forget the feeling when I first entered the building of a corporate machine the size of Ray-Jay. It reeked of wealth, prestige, and the ambiance like nothing I had ever encountered at that point of my life. There were six towers and at the time had the largest privately owned art collection in North America. My only work experience at that point in my life, had been working 9 years at a Taco Bell! I felt like I didn't belong or have a chance at the job, truly, I was intimidated.

There were three stages to the interview process. The second stage consisted of a 25 question exam type format with very specific questions regarding groups of numbers. Abnormalities were to be found and identified and the exam was timed at 45 minutes. When the 45 minutes was up, I had completed an embarrassing six questions. I nearly excused myself to the bathroom as quickly as I could but sucked it up and handed it in. The reaction from human resources was completely void of emotion as I was told "we will contact you if we are interested." My ego had been crushed.

A few days later, I got a call from human resources requesting my availability for another interview. My assumption was that they had me mixed up with someone else and I would be like Charlie Brown running up to the football, only to have it snatched away and be informed of the mix up when I arrived. Low and behold I was greeted by the supervisor of the Purchase and Sales Department and another interview was conducted.

For whatever reason, the interview went smoothly and I was offered a position with the Purchase and Sales Department as a Comparison Clerk. I had absolutely no clue what qualified me for the position, had zero financial degrees or experience, and was still convinced he thought he was interviewing someone else. When the moment came for me to accept the position, I had to confront what seemed to be the error in the offer based on my six questions answered before this got any more embarrassing. He then told me in fact yes he had the right person and that I had answered all six questions with 100% accuracy. It turned out all the other applicants had rushed to answer as many questions as possible and in so doing lost the ability to be accurate. They weren't looking for all the questions to be answered, they were concerned with the attention to detail.

My job was to be in at 7:30 a.m. I'd have a report of all NASDAQ trades with Ray-Jay and other financial broker dealers like Merrill Lynch, Goldman Sachs, Smith Barney, all the big boys. My report was always dealing with yesterday's trades and finding the "trade break" that prevented a stock from properly settling and commodities being distributed amongst the corporate giants. The market opened at 9:30 a.m. so I had two full hours to complete my task, find the "trade breaks", and report them to the trading floor before the market opened. It made everyone's job easier the sooner I got the "breaks" to the trading floor because once the market opened my associates were focused on that day's business at hand, not yesterdays. I was essentially the checks and balances for millions of dollars to be reconciled so my job was crucially important and attention to detail was the backbone.

I mentioned before I have OCD and there are a variety of ways in which it manifests itself. One of my idiosyncratic behaviors is that I would separate words in my head as they would be typed onto a keyboard, alphabetize them, then say them three times in my head but only if they were under 10 letters. Just take the word table and picture what hand would type it on a keyboard. L=right hand, ABET=left hand.

I would randomly seek words I had never yet mastered when in conversations or reading, and my mind became like a machine constantly processing this formula.

That was just letters, numbers were another fascination my mind seemed to be obsessed with. Any numbers I saw, license plates, billboards, telephone numbers, grocery store prices, had to be added. I would count essentially anything while driving such as the yellow lines, or telephone poles. Once I was hired at Ray-Jay, my whole job consisted of solving number problems. What had been mentally exhausting much of my life, was actually now paying my bills.

One of the valuable lessons I learned at Ray-Jay is that I was an effective communicator. On a daily basis I was talking with other financial broker dealers with people who represented their institutions financial interests just as I did for Ray-Jay. Quickly it became clear to me that once I learned my job duties, I developed confidence in my position. I learned my personality, attitude, intellect, and humor all came together and it was as if a magic elixir had been captured.

I was a rising star in corporate America and it was getting the attention of some of the most beautiful women I had ever been around as well as the bosses on the trading floor. I was being recruited by the NASDAQ machine just as the internet was exploding, and continued to become enamored by all the bells and whistles this fast-paced life seemed to be providing. Many of the bosses that were attempting to recruit me that I interacted with were female. I was frequently being "called to their offices" and let's just say it was on and popping! There almost seemed to be a competition of one wanting to be better than the next, it was absolutely intoxicating. What was so flattering to my ego, is that none of these women were advancing their careers by sleeping with me. I had a confidence and swagger that I couldn't have possibly perceived existed inside me.

As I was in this phase of my life, I was a single dad. I had recently agreed to move a high school friend who was currently separated from her husband to rent my third bedroom. It didn't take long before we were having sex and my first introduction to crack cocaine soon followed. I can go some many different ways with the story here, but I want to continue to focus on explaining every carnal and hedonistic over indulgence I could consume, was being saturated.

I can't tell you how many times I have chased anything that felt good in the moment and completely disregarded the way it would be impacting my future. There were no concepts of long-term goals, only fulfilling my urges, desires, and laying the blueprint for failure.

Everyday I went back to the trading floor after the market closed for any final business I may have had to wrap up. Much of what I was walking into was completely contingent upon how their trading day went. The same people who at the beginning of the day were on top of the world, full of energy, and charismatic, had done a complete 180. By the end of some days, it looked as if someone had died or they were staring at some distant tragedy.

There was a complete absence of the spiritual realm (in a positive way) having any impact on my life. It's always been something that's puzzled me about atheists or agnostics, there doesn't seem to be a doubt or debate on evil's existence?

However, there seems to be widespread acceptance of natural laws governing our world including everything having an opposite. So if evil exists, it brings up two natural questions to me?

1. Who or what is in charge of this "evil"?

2. What would be on the opposite end of evil presupposing everything has an opposite?

At this point I'd like to mention something I heard on Dr. Andrew Huberman's podcast. Doctor Huberman is a brilliant man who works at Stanford University and studies neurobiology. On this particular podcast, he was interviewing Dr. Anna Lembke on her Dopamine Nation book I've mentioned before. She mentioned people in recovery are like modern day prophets when implementing their twelve step program. It gave me the idea for the title of this chapter as I contrast it to my experience at Ray-Jay in corporate America. Bottom line, if I put my energy into temporary things such as money, drugs, sex, food, gambling, I will only get temporary satisfaction.

On one end Modern Day Profit (our flesh) represents much of the defect side of our characteristics and attributes. Conversely, Modern Day Prophet (spiritual), is the implementation and concentration on God to cultivate our assets. Interestingly, this satisfies the universal law of substitution which simply put states nature abhors a vacuum. When we remove the defect, something must go in that hole. This is where we focus on our assets. Using the 7 deadly sins as a reference point for this list I submit the following:

    Defect (flesh)   Asset (spirit)

Pride	Humility
Anger	Peace/joy
Greed	Generosity
Lust	Chastity
Envy	Contentment
Gluttony	Moderation
Sloth	Energy

I've noticed when I concentrate on the assets, my defects aren't as rooted. One of the main effects of this is I stop trying to manipulate outcomes. I was very good at it, and still am. However, when has getting what I want ever been good for me?

I'd like to share what I believe to be one of if not the greatest perspectives on how we as human beings can treat one another. This was written by Saint Francis of Assisi.

"Lord, make me a channel of thy peace;
that where there is hatred, I may bring love;

That where there is wrong, I may bring the spirit of forgiveness;

That where there is discord, I may bring harmony;

That where there is error, I may bring truth;

That where there is doubt, I may bring faith;

That where there is despair, I may bring hope;

That where there are shadows, I may bring light;

That where there is sadness, I may bring joy;

Lord, grant that I may seek rather to comfort, than to be comforted;

To understand rather than to be understood;

To love, then to be loved for it is by self forgetting that one finds;

It is by forgiving, that one is forgiven;

It is by dying, that one awakens to eternal life"

Proverbs 3: 5,6
Trust in the Lord with all your heart and lean not on your own understanding, and all your ways acknowledge him, and he will make your paths straight.

Focus on the spiritual realm, our assets, by going to God. It's always the answer, we have a direct line. Trust and remember that there is perfection in the design.

Chapter 3

JAGGED EDGE

My father was the wisest and most understanding man I ever met in my life. My mom and dad divorced when I was 7, but my father was always in my life, however, not present. He was my biggest fan, counselor, and critic when needed. He was able to immediately detect when I was bullshitting him, and myself. As a result, he not only knew about my addiction but I had the benefit of getting and staying honest with him throughout my active addiction.

After years of chronic relapses, rebuilding my life only to tear it down again, a clear behavioral pattern had firmly rooted. It broke my heart when I would finally resurface, to tell him I had done it again. While I was on a binge my phone would ring and I'd see it was my dad calling and not answer or shut the phone off. I can feel the pain as I write this, now that I'm not numb, as to the hell any parent must feel not knowing if their child is in jail, the hospital, dead or alive.

My father was in corporate America for the last 20 years or so of his career. He sold banking systems on a global scale to all the major banks. If there was an issue with a contract being finalized or prevented from closing, it was referred to as a "Jagged Edge." A jagged edge could also be anything in life that needed fixing or life issue that prevented growth. My dad would listen to me explain my most recent brilliant deductions for "this" relapse. He would point out to me that the reason always seemed to change or morph into something else. He would also show me the reason I had deduced last time was yet again obviously wrong, because here we are again. Dad said to me " son this addiction is a jagged edge, and it's only a matter of time before you die or something terrible is going to happen."

On April 14th 2008, I had been up for 3 days on a crack binge and needed to come down. I went to a liquor store and it had not opened yet. Make a mental note to yourself by the way, if you ever find yourself at a liquor store BEFORE IT OPENS, your life is officially off the rails! I bought a half gallon of vodka and returned to the residence of my new acquaintance and we began drinking. My intention was to drink enough to pass out but for whatever reason it gave me new life and we decided it was time to get high again.

My car's gas tank was empty, but her car was a viable option and I went out to go score some dope. My options close by didn't pan out so I went 15 miles away in a mostly blacked-out state. On the way back I recall pulling up into a left turn lane at a red light. I looked around, saw no cars, and turned left while the arrow was still red. I didn't finish the turn before a Pinellas county sheriff pulled up behind me and threw his lights on. I pulled off onto the shoulder and shut the car off. As the officer approached my vehicle, I'll never forget the feeling of complete defiance and disregard for their authority. I waited until he got even with my back bumper, looked in the rear view mirror, and thought "not today." I restarted the car and punched the gas. I found out later I had been clocked at 92 miles per hour and accelerating so the pursuit was over before it began.

The next 20 minutes or so I have absolutely no memory of whatsoever. However as I'm sure you can relate, whenever there is an extreme adrenaline rush involved, details after the fact seem to be recalled. I was a little less than 2 miles from getting back to my new acquaintance and I remember taking a big drink of my vodka and orange juice as I got into another left turn lane. The next thing I know, I've run into the back of a civilian vehicle and smashed the front end of the Mitsubishi Galant like an accordion. I glanced to my right and two lanes over was a Largo police vehicle.

At this point my adrenaline took off like a rocket and in my panic I cut through a liquor store parking lot. The cop quickly pursued but I knew these little neighborhoods and streets like the back of my hand and lost him fairly quickly. It's usually at this point of the story someone will ask "why didn't you just park the car and leave it?" In hindsight, of course this would have been the thing to do, after all, I had gotten away. However, it's applying logic to a situation that by its very nature is illogical. I was absolutely out of control.

All I can remember thinking is I'm so close to where I'm headed, just get there. As I came around the final corner to my destination, the Galant looked like it belonged on the Island of Misfit Toys. Parked in front of the driveway where I was headed, were three Pinellas county sheriff vehicles. I decided to punch it!

What I later discovered was as a result of the first fleeing and eluding, the officer had gotten the license plate number off the Galant before he exited his car to approach me. Because I took off, of course he radioed in the tag number to dispatch and the three cruisers I am now flying past were sent to the address the tag was registered to. My new acquaintance, being questioned by the police as to the car's whereabouts no doubt said she knew nothing.

I think the turning of heads towards the Galant as I flew by could have won an Olympic gold for its synchronization. The missing vehicle had just been found! I again made the brilliant decision to keep running, I flew through a stop sign and nearly ran into the Largo cop I had just gotten away from. As I looked in the rear view mirror all three cruisers activated their lights and sirens and pursued.

I began zigzagging through streets and eventually reached a stop sign, yes I stopped. One of the cruisers pulled up parallel to my car. I attempted to turn left. The cop scooted forward as I attempted my turn and our cars made contact with one another. Realizing my efforts were futile, I turned right and the pursuit continued. This exact same scenario occurred at the next stop sign just a mile ahead. As I continued to flee, up to this point there had been no other traffic on the streets. However, the street I was on now was a different story and about a half mile ahead was a major intersection.

I recall reaching for my drink and the next thing I knew my car was facing the opposite direction on the shoulder, on the opposite side of the road. A perfectly executed PIT maneuver had been done to my car. As a result of the PIT maneuver, my car stalled and two cruisers pulled in front of my car creating essentially a perfect V shape. Everything I just described happened in a flash. In my panic, I tried to restart my car. I quickly realized it wouldn't start because the car was still in drive from the PIT maneuver.

From your own experience, I'm sure you know a car won't start when the transmission is in drive. It needed to be put back in park. I did so, reengaged the engine, and when I looked up, the officer who performed the PIT maneuver was standing a few feet in front of my car with his gun pointed right at me. Later, at deposition, the officer stated: "Mr George made eye contact with me, yelled fuck you, restarted his vehicle, and stepped on the gas." To this day, I have no idea if I said that, but I do remember stepping on the gas.

The Galant had front wheel drive and because I was on a shoulder in Florida it was basically sand. I hit the gas so hard that the dirt began rooster tailing under the front tires. Eventually, the tires grabbed traction and my car catapulted forward directly at the cop. He later explained he had a split second decision to make. He could have shot me through the windshield but there was no guarantee my foot would come off the gas and the accelerating vehicle would pin him against his car; Or, do what he did, which is jump on the hood of his cruiser as my car slammed into his cruiser barely missing him. In fact, it was so close, that 18 months later at deposition, the officer showed my attorney the mark on his right boot where my front bumper made contact as he jumped backward to avoid the impact. My car collided with his cruiser with such force that it ricocheted into the other cruiser that had formed the V shape in an attempt to block me off.

What I had no knowledge of, is a third car had taken position 10 feet behind me as this whole situation was unfolding. All of my attention was in front of me, not behind me. From the vantage point of the officer behind me, he's obviously observing all of this in front of him and only sees my car lunge forward as his fellow officer flew on to the hood. He justifiably thought I had used my car to run down this officer. As a result, he gave the order "officer down shoot to kill!" Simultaneously, as he attempted to get out of his vehicle, I had put my car in reverse and punched the gas to get away from the two cruisers I had just slammed into. I hit the driver side door of the officer behind me who had just given the order to kill me, pinning him in his vehicle. Realizing I was trapped, I pulled the car forward, shut it off, and threw the keys out the window. I was hit in my head harder than I've ever been hit in my life by an elbow, pulled out of the driver side window, and kicked to sleep.

It turns out the only reason I actually hadn't been shot is an unbelievable story. The officer who had given the order to shoot to kill, had trouble getting out split seconds before I slammed into him, why? His normal cruiser just happened to be getting an oil change that day so he had a replacement cruiser. The significance of that is his replacement vehicle didn't have the automatic locking switch on his armrest. As he was attempting to get out of his vehicle, he was reaching for an armrest switch that wasn't there. He had to manually unlock his door, and in this nanosecond of discovery, he couldn't get out to kill me in time before I slammed into his door..

I was originally charged with the following:

4 counts of Aggravated Battery on LEO
1 count of Attempted Murder in the second degree
3 counts of Fleeing and Eluding
1 count of Resisting arrest with violence
1 count DUI
1 count leaving the scene of an accident with damage

The level of my intoxication was ridiculously high. I blew a .19 nearly 4 hours after the incident. The legal limit in Florida is .08. Little did I know as the arrest affidavit was being filled out, the attempted second degree murder had been modified from attempted murder of a LEO, which is punishable by life. Eventually, the attempted murder in the second degree was reduced to aggravated assault on a LEO. I sat in the Pinellas county jail for 34 months before my plea happened, I received 12 years in prison. In Florida, there is a statute that mandates an inmate must do 85% of their total sentence. For me, 12 years breaks down to 10 years, 2 months, and 9 days.

To say I was horrified on every level is an understatement. I was about to embark on something hundreds of people told me that heard my story. "There's no way I could do 12 years in prison." Let me tell you, you have no idea what you're capable of, until you're forced to have to do it. I had begun a journey reconnecting with God the whole time I was awaiting my fate from that night. Many of my prayers were still what would be referred to as "Fox hole praying." This is a term used to identify soldiers in battle who felt death was imminent and began begging God to spare their life.

You see, I would pray to God and ask for His will, but then I would tell Him what that needs to look like. I was still nowhere near a point of surrender from my own free will. Free will is a topic unto itself that could take up an entire book. It's like a knife, in the hands of a burglar it's a deadly weapon, however, in the hands of a surgeon it's a life-saving tool. God loves me enough to allow me to implement my free will and even to reject him. I needed the strength to go on and God was allowing me to go through the trial of my life and let me willingly depend and trust Him.

My mind kept trying to process the prison sentence I had just received. I was learning that strength does not come from winning. Your struggles develop your strengths. When you go through hardships and decide not to surrender, that is strength! Yet in this case I needed to surrender- my will- in order to win and allow pain to be a pivot.

There was a Lebanese prophet named Khalil Kabron that is quoted saying "pain is but the breaking of a shell which leads to understanding."

What we do with any hardship, real or perceived, is a choice. How could I possibly endure this prison sentence? Several scriptures were revealed to me because I felt the presence of an energy I can only describe as a connection with the spiritual realm. God was interacting with me in my life because I put my hand in His.

John 3:30
He must increase, but I must decrease

My interpretation, the spirit of God and my understanding of that connectivity must elevate. My humanness, my free will, needed to submit.

Romans 8:28
We know that all things work together for good for those who love God, who are called according to His purpose.

In less than 10 seconds, my life had been spared twice. Once from the officer I charged at with the car and he chose to jump. Secondly, by an act of what I believe was God's intervention, the officer's car just happened to be a replacement vehicle on that day. No one can tell me God didn't put a hedge of protection around me and all those involved. You will see as this book unfolds, there have been several moments that could have ended my life. In some cases it actually did, but here I am. It is incumbent upon me to share these stories because quite honestly, I still want to get high. What keeps me going is that one person may read this and it keeps them clean and they go to God. My life and those closest to me have been hijacked by my poor choices and what were merely moments. Holidays, birthdays, graduations, family functions and funerals have all negatively been impacted by my lack of presence. Don't let a moment dictate the momentum of your life.

Chapter 4

ADDITION BY SUBTRACTION

Being shipped off to prison is an experience that will be virtually impossible to articulate. Up to this point, I had been in the county jail for just shy of 3 years. While in the county and knowing this day was inevitably coming, there was an accumulation of information on what to expect. However, as with any experience, nothing can truly prepare you for the real event. I was anticipating everything from the officers whipping our asses, or being ready to fight or "bump."

While in the County jail, I was no longer "fox hole praying", but developed a dialogue with God that was available at any time. The energy and feedback being received from this dialogue with God, I can only explain as mathematical, which given my proclivity towards numbers, I suppose makes sense. It was being shown to me that in order to grow I needed to eliminate a lot of baggage, belief systems, and attitudes. It was time to get honest about my thinking and decision making.

Said another way, we can add to our life, by subtracting things from it. Prison was going to be an environment where many things were subtracted. I was about to enter a habitat that was the complete antithesis of freedom. Everything from what time the lights go off and on, when you eat, what you eat, what you can wear, what time you can use the phone, visitation, where those visitors will sit, the amount of pictures you're allowed, when your laundry will be done, when you can go outside, what job function you will have, the location of your bunk, when you can get supplies like soap and toilet paper. The internal processes of trying to get anything done like adding a person to your visitation or phone list, would make our political system look efficient in comparison.

From October through April a very thin collared jacket was provided and in the Florida prison system there are only heaters in the dorms. The temperatures must be at an undisclosed projected number before that heater is turned on. Thin sheets and oftentimes a recycled blanket with holes in it is what we were provided to stay warm. In Florida it's hot with tropical humidity, however, there is no air conditioning or climate control. Ceiling fans are in the dorms and it's not uncommon for officers to attempt to control our behavior and punish us by turning them off and on.

Depending on your classification status, you are either in a two-man cell or what's referred to as an "open bay." Open bay dorms can have anywhere from 70 to 100 people on one side of a dorm with a mix of single and double bunks. There's only three feet of space between bunks and all your belongings must fit in a foot locker. If you share a double bunk, it's like your typical bunk bed, except only 30 inches wide and the person you must endure this with is referred to as your "bunkie."

There are several directions I can go with the story and I understand there is a fascination with prison to those who haven't been. The prison system is infested with drugs, although while I was in the 2 main drugs were K2 and Suboxone. My entire prison bid I stayed clean and the obsession to use was no longer with me. There was nothing that was going to affect my ability to get out as fast as I could and getting caught with any drugs would have backed up my gain time. It was quite common to go to the bathroom and see people passed out on toilets, or passing K2 sticks around. There is no privacy when using the bathroom and when sitting down, if you're next to someone your knees are within inches of one another, absolutely no privacy.

What I want to focus on is that it was during this 10-year prison bid there was nothing but a complete disconnect from society and life. I was forced to ask myself "How do I get through this?" If my thoughts and behavior got me here, everything needed to be challenged. What do I believe about anything and why? Most importantly, what are my beliefs about God and what is my connection to God?

Prison was giving me the chance to add to my life and subtract what needed to be removed. During my incarceration I read countless books, both fiction for entertainment and escape, but also any spiritual books I could get my hands on. As I began reading books like Conversations with God (Neale Donald Walsch), The Power of Now, A New Heaven and a New Earth (Eckhart Tolle), The Untethered Soul (Michael Singer), it became clear to me that my thirst for the spiritual realm was being quenched. Something was appealing to my intellect and spirit and it was giving me peace.

The other thing it was doing is it moved me further and further away from the mandates of Christianity. There was nothing overly slanderous or bashing of Christianity, but there was no mention of a savior much less the need for one. Everything I needed was already apparently in me and "I" was all that needed cultivating. Specific attention and importance was given to different states of being. Higher states of consciousness, awareness, and mindfulness were all keys to inner freedom. It was all so convincing and interesting that I had to now disprove my Christian roots by finding material to delegitimize the Bible. I will discuss this more in the chapter "Came To Believe" later in the book. The main reason much of the spiritual material I was reading appealed to me, is I was realizing how much of a problem I had with authority. I perceived Christianity as a threat because it had only one way to God and that was through Jesus and Jesus alone.

As I continued to grow spiritually, the prison camp I had been sent to was Tomoka Correctional in Daytona Beach. Virtually all Florida prisons have a work camp on the premises although usually acres and acres separate the work camps from the main units. Work camps are significantly smaller than main units and have contracts with their respective county's Department of Transportation or Public Works. Any guys you see mowing the grass or weed whacking ditches in blue uniforms with white stripes down the pant leg, belong to the Florida Department of Corrections. Inmates with low custody levels are "permitted" to go out and work their asses off to avoid getting put in confinement for refusing to work. Oftentimes the boots provided by the prison system don't fit, the soles are gone or there's holes in them. Guys are mandated to deal with mosquitoes, water moccasins, and any other Florida critter while the officer in charge of that crew sits in a climate controlled truck "supervising." I can't tell you how grateful any inmate would be to have their family provide some real boots that can be bought and at least make it a little more comfortable. The prison system makes money being contracted with the Department of Transportation and Public Works, so they use the inmates for free labor. It's modern day slavery.

My custody level never permitted me the alleged honor of going outside the gate. This left very few work options for me. However, shortly after my arrival at Tomoka, I began noticing inmates with dogs on the compound. After 3 weeks of working in the kitchen, I was eligible to be in the dog program and one of the reasons was that I still had six plus years to go before my release. It was desirable for long-term inmates to be selected, because it provided an opportunity to become a better trainer and teach other inmates.

The Prison Pups N Pals dog program had two inmates assigned to each dog; a caretaker and a trainer. There were 10 dogs in the program as well as a lead instructor and an assistant lead instructor for a total of 22 inmates. Our dogs came in from a local shelter and we trained as a group for 1 hour, 5 days a week, for 8 weeks. During the 8 week training period the goal was to adopt each dog to their "forever home" using social media run by the prison. We had two civilian facilitators who came in and taught our curriculum which were the basic obedience commands: sit, down, stay, come, heel, front, and stand. Additionally, there was a program within the program called Paws of Freedom. Two dogs from each group stayed back for 8 more weeks of training to be paired with a veteran. I was moved as I listened to veterans share their daily struggles and challenges. I became inspired by the cause and felt privileged to be a part of it. I was beginning to see how dogs were changing lives and giving hope to Veterans in need.

As the process of training continued, it was common for potential adopters to come and meet the dog or view the dog in class. It was so refreshing to see a civilian and be able to interact, but the officer in charge of the program was always present during this interaction. Our mere presence was always scrutinized with an air of suspicion. It was a reminder that any inmate was constantly viewed as a threat by the prison system.

I was incarcerated from 04-14-2008 thru 06-23-2018. During this time there was no contact from my older son. I would send letters to my mom and sister to give to him, but there was never a response. My younger son and I stayed in touch through letters and I was legally married during my incarceration, however, there was no marriage. My actions had allowed all these possibilities to exist and I was reaping what I had sewn. My father and I had gotten the closest we had ever been in our lives. Every Saturday during my prison bid, I would call my dad and we had 15 minutes per call before the system disconnected the call. If for any reason I missed calling on a Saturday, I was quickly reminded of this on my next call. It provided reassurance and comfort to my dad that his son had made it another week and that our voices were heard by one another.

On one particular call, I could immediately tell something was wrong. My dad could barely speak, he was openly weeping. When he collected himself to talk, he informed me that one of my younger brothers, Chris, had committed suicide by shooting himself. The complete and total agony of any parent losing their child is one of if not the greatest tragedies and fears in life. It's just not the natural progression of our concepts of life and death, certainly as a parent - we are not supposed to bury our children. Not only was my dad in mourning, but he was having to be the one to tell me my brother had died. It put him in an impossible position to ever prepare for in life. He was such a caring and loving father that he was concerned for my emotional well-being and how I would take this being in prison. There are no provisions or allowances for funerals to be attended to by inmates- NONE. So there was another layer of reality to contend with, I couldn't be there for my family in a time of need.

Within a year of Chris passing, my grandfather passed away at 101 years old from skin cancer. He was a prominent doctor who had moved his practice from Maryland to Las Vegas before Vegas was as we know it now. He was completely cogent and could carry on a conversation with the best of them until the very end. He was interviewed by the local Vegas media when he turned 100 and as a centenarian was asked "How did you make it to 100 years old?" His answer obviously warrants merit. He answered, "As a doctor, you may find it surprising that it has very little to do with diet or exercise. It has to do with your mental state and having no regrets. Learn from your mistakes and serve others."

This advice could not have been more relevant as I found myself in the mothership of all timeouts. Through dog training, I began to see the relevance of serving others and how edifying for the soul it had become. Watching these dogs leave every 8 weeks was so bittersweet. On one hand, I had completed a job well done and handing the dog off to its new owner and forever home was satisfying. On the other hand, some of the dogs were literally all I felt like I had on Thanksgiving and Christmas, and were there for me to cope with the deaths in my family. Those dogs were there for me in a way nothing else could be. Many of them have a very special place in my heart because no matter my mood, the dog was always consistent. They were teaching me as much as I was teaching them. Life isn't a matter of having what I want, but wanting what I have. Dogs were teaching me that in their contentment, was peace.

Something else I noticed during this time is how much more confident I became with the dogs. The dogs were responding to me in a positive way because of their respect for me. The dogs helped give me back confidence in myself and we were functioning as a unit. Tone of voice, body language, and facial expression are the 3 main keys to dog training. Within that communication an energy, trust, and bond is created.

The last 3 years I was at Tomoka, I became the lead instructor of the dog program. By this time, our program had become well ingrained and our civilian facilitators needed only to supervise our training. My responsibility was to instruct class 5 days a week and be aware of how all the dogs in our program were progressing. This also included being in charge of the inmates in the program. It was the greatest hands-on training for any type of management position you could imagine. It's a slippery slope being in charge of anything in prison because we are all equal. I'm just an inmate like every other guy in there. However, we were held to a higher standard because we were in a program and I was dealing with guys that had heavy charges just like me. Prison taught me many things and one of them is that you can say almost anything to anybody, so long as you allow them their dignity. At times, it presented significant challenges having to put out fires, prevent fights from happening, and problem solving in very emotionally charged situations. Some of the guys had manslaughter, burglary, arm robbery, you name it. They had established good behavior for years and earned the right to be in that program. I watched incredible transformations of men, simply by being able to interact with a dog.

The last year of my incarceration was spent at a work release facility. During that time inmates are permitted to work out in society while saving money to reenter society. I worked at an oyster bar as a short order cook. Over the course of the year I was able to save $15,000. Just before I left Tomoka, a curriculum for our dog program was approved by the state. 3700 hours was the maximum number of hours recognized by the state of Florida for dog training. I had been doing it for so long that I had logged over 10,000 dog training hours. Shortly before my release, I was mailed 4 state certifications through the Department of Education for dog training. Little did I know, God was preparing me for my future.

This chapter has been difficult to write for many reasons. Reflecting on prison triggers my PTSD. I got PTSD as a result of prison and I'm sure many of you can understand why. For the sake of staying on topic and moving the story along, I omitted dozens of stories that I could have shared. Many of those involved tremendous violence I witnessed and even some deaths. I couldn't have survived prison without God. Although I was being misguided by the spiritual material I was reading, at the time I believed what I had been digesting because I felt something. There's no doubt I was connecting to God in some way. My dad gave me one of the greatest compliments I've ever received in my life when he told me "son, you came out better than you went in." My younger son Taylor and I reconnected about 2 years before my release. As I was about to reenter society, he was entering his junior year in high school.

Chapter 5

THE GOOD SHEPHERD

After my release from prison, my main goal was to reconnect with Taylor and get him through the rest of High School. We had begun talking again roughly 2 years before my release as a result of my dad bringing Taylor to see me in prison. When we originally reunited, I hadn't seen Taylor for 7 years. Taylor was in an environment with his mother as well as numerous uncles and drugs were just part of the scene. Fortunately, to his credit, he managed to stay away from those early teen pitfalls and traps. I felt compelled and responsible to get Taylor out of his situation and allow him an opportunity and a fighting chance to find a life. After all, I owed it to him as his father. It was as a result of my actions that his situation was a reality. I wasn't present to protect and provide and he was paying a price for my absence through no fault of his own.

I didn't have the time, money, or energy after 10 years in prison to attempt a custody battle. Quite frankly, my odds didn't seem great considering where I had been to think any judge would just grant me custody. The path of least resistance was to have them both come with me. My intention was never to reconcile the marriage, but to provide an opportunity for Taylor to have both his parents. At least I had the $15,000 to start over with and as dysfunctional as it may sound, Taylor would be with his mom and dad under one roof.

When anyone is starting over in life, especially when getting out of prison, you will need three things: somewhere to live, somewhere to work, and transportation. Days before my release from the work release facility, I had secured an Airbnb for the first 10 days on Indian Rocks Beach in Pinellas county. After my dad picked me up on my release date, my first real meal on the outside in 10 years was at a Cracker Barrel. The next stop was to open a bank account with Wells Fargo and I used $300 to obtain what's called a secured credit card. I highly recommend this to anyone being released from prison to begin rebuilding your credit. The $300 becomes your credit limit and it reports to all the major credit bureaus every month. After 6 months of on time payments, the card "graduates" from secured to unsecured AND you get your $300 back. As a result of opening the checking account with the remaining funds, a temporary debit card was issued on the spot.

My next stop was to the DMV where I owed roughly $700 to reinstate my driver's license. I discovered the only rental car company to take a temporary debit card was Enterprise. Since I now had my son and wife and all their belongings, I got an SUV for a week.

I had a phone because I had the benefit of re-entering society from work release. Prior to my release, I made sure all my necessary "ducks were in a row" so I knew on day one where I was going and what needed to be done. Being the loving father he was, my dad paid for the Airbnb as a gift to help me out. So on day 1 of my release I had a rental cottage on the beach, my driver's license back, a bank account opened, a secured credit card, a temporary debit card, an SUV, along with my son and his mom.

I could at least breathe now but securing housing, where to work, and permanent transportation quickly took priority. I found reasonably priced temporary rentals roughly 2 hours away on an online rental site in The Villages. The Villages is a retirement community in Central Florida that is equivalent to Disney World for adults. Everything is golf cart accessible, and tailored to its folks on the back nine so to speak, with countless activities to remain connected to life. Many of The Villages residents are gone for several months out of the year, typically in the summer, and their homes sit vacant. As a result, those residents allow their homes to be rented out through a property management company. Fortunately, I discovered this safe haven at the right time of year as these rentals are about a third of the price than what they rent out for in the winter. All they wanted was the money to secure the temporary rental, no background checks.

I secured a temporary rental for $1,400 a month for the months of July and August and used this opportunity to jump to the next lily pad of my reentry into the real world. During these two months I bought a 15-year-old Nissan Altima, five speed, with 140,000 mi on it, for $1,500. One of the "big three needs" had been secured - transportation. I was blasting out resumes like crazy mostly on Indeed as there was ever looming pressure that more permanent housing still needed to be secured.

I was completely on my own financially to be the bearer of all responsibility. Also on the horizon was my son needing to be put in a school for his Junior year. I took any job that would hire me. What did that look like? 1. Setting up three golf courses first thing in the morning by moving the pin placement on all the greens. 2. Worked at a car wash 3. Dishwashing at a Bonefish Grill-all paid minimum wage.

By now, I'm a month out of prison in a fully furnished beautiful three bedroom rental in The Villages. However, this place wasn't sustainable and none of these jobs were going to be taking me to the next level. One positive that did occur, as a result of my secured credit card having its first on time payment, my credit score appeared on credit karma at 630. I suppose it's looking at the glass half full, but one benefit of being off grid for all those years was my credit had essentially been wiped clean. This was the first reporting of any kind under my name to a credit bureau in over 10 years.

While I had been working three part-time dead-end jobs, I never stopped submitting my resume. Any job that I thought might give me an interview I sent an application to. I was a few weeks into this process, when jobs for animal care, or anything dog related got my attention. Any online job search site like Indeed will give you an option for a cover letter. The cover letter simply allows you an opportunity to be your initial introduction to any potential employer. So as I began noticing dog training positions within a reasonable radius of my Villages rental, I thought why not try?

I created a cover letter that was completely transparent in which I acknowledged immediately that I was a certified dog trainer in Florida. They were through the Department of Education, but all my certifications were obtained while in the Department of Corrections. I can't express the importance of this step because now if any potentially interested employer contacted me they already know I'm a convicted felon, and I've done time.

It was now late August and the time frame for the rental in The Villages was about to expire. There was the added pressure of having a 17 year old in an age restricted retirement community and needing to secure Taylor at a school - we needed to get out. The property management company in charge of the rental said they had family friendly rentals just outside the jurisdiction of The Villages. There were only two actually, and the cheapest one rented for $1,800 requiring first month, last month, and security deposit as well as a year lease. All I had was a one month on time payment with my secured credit card, three part-time minimum wage jobs, and of course the rental required an application. The only thing going for me was I still had enough to cover the $5400 it would take to move in. There's no way given the normal landscape of how the real world works that this formula was going to pay dividends.

It was going to be impossible to keep my criminal record hidden from a property management company on a rental application. It seemed easy to be transparent on an Indeed cover letter and hitting the submit button to an unknown person who I would never see or talk to if rejected. This next step however involved the property management representative walking me around a four bedroom, 2,500 sq ft, two car garage home, it was beautiful!

When it came time for the representative to ask for the application details, all I could do was be completely honest and totally transparent. I mean really it was all going to come out anyway right? I explained I had just gotten out of prison due to having a substance abuse problem. I went on to share that I was clean now for over 10 years, although in fairness, all that clean time was in prison and I've only been out for 2 months. The jobs I had were all part-time, but I had the first month and last month, and a security deposit that I could pay. I'll never forget looking her in the eye and saying "I'll make it work, I just need a chance."

It turns out the representative's brother had a background also and I could see immediately her face begin to soften. It was never revealed to me what the background issue was, but there was no doubt an emotional connection had been made. However, at the end of the day, this was still a business and boxes needed to be checked - after all emotional connections don't pay the rent. She asked me if anyone would co-sign for the lease? My dad would have been the only one, but the fact that she was asking seemed promising. She told me if I could find a cosigner she would try and push the application through.

My father's health had not been well, however, he had just beaten prostate cancer. As I mentioned before, he had lost a child to suicide as well as his father while I was in prison. It was hard for me to even ask my dad for help, did I have a right? Immediately he told me yes he would do it, but only for one year. It was at that time I expressed my concerns of my ability to sustain it due to my lack of sufficient income or job prospects. He said matter of factly to me "son I believe in you." Once my Dad's credit was pulled and adding him as a cosigner, the representative from the rental company informed me the application was approved.

Within the first two weeks of moving in, I got a voicemail from a dog training organization GAMSD, wanting to conduct a phone interview. Keep in mind I knew because of my inclusive cover letter of how I obtained my certifications this had to be a legitimate inquiry. Preliminary questions of my experience were discussed and I asked for confirmation and my own reassurance "you see where my certifications came from?" There was just a brief acknowledgement of "yes we do," and I was asked if I could come in for a working interview.

The location of GAMSD was exactly 60 miles one way, but it was all interstate and a four-lane highway. It was a beautiful drive through Marion county once I was on highway 27 as it snakes through horse country and into Levy county. I can remember the feeling of complete freedom as I took in the surrounding landscape. As I arrived at GAMSD there was a feeling of trepidation and an overall sense of nervousness. Doubt began to creep in and I became paralyzed in the car. You see GAMSD stands for: Guardian Angels Medical Service Dogs. They provide German Shepherds as service dogs to veterans.

Yes I was impressive on paper with my four state certifications, however, these weren't just dogs, they were service animals. In Florida, only two animals are recognized as service animals: dogs and miniature horses. A service animal by law is an animal that performs "tasks" for a person with a disability. Those tasks must be directly related to that person's disability.

As I shut the car off my hands seemed frozen to the keys as they stayed in the ignition. What in the world made me think I had the qualifications for a medical service dog training facility? Immediately, after asking the question, it was as if something came into my stream of consciousness.

Psalm 46:10 Be still and know that I am God

Recollections of being hired at Ray-Jay when I thought there was no chance came to mind. And then, the Paws of Freedom program while I was in prison pairing dogs with veterans had been preparing me for this opportunity. God was revealing to me with crystal clear precision how those 10 years in prison had been laying the groundwork for this exact moment. I got out of the car with chill bumps and tears of gratitude in my eyes.

The interview was conducted by three individuals, two of them were ex-military. It felt very formal, structured, and robotic in its delivery. All of the questions I nailed with confidence and I was in my comfort zone talking about dogs as well as having managed people. Nothing about my incarceration was mentioned and eventually the interview moved to a Hands-On portion with only one of the three interviewers being present.

At this point I hadn't worked a dog in about 15 months, but as you can identify, if you're skilled in what you do it's practically muscle memory. I'll never forget when a beautiful 18 month old female German Shepherd was brought out and anything that was asked of us was performed with flawless execution. It felt as if this dog and I had been dancing partners all our lives.

After the working part of the interview was over, I went back inside to where the earlier part of the interview had been conducted. Only the program director was present now and I saw a brief thumbs up from the individual I did the working portion of the interview with as he exited the room. The director looked at me briefly, then to his desk, and he said "Why did you go to prison?"

The ebb and flow of the last hour was nerve-racking to say the least. I had forgotten all about the anxiety while frozen in the car horrified by this exact moment. Before I could think, it was as if some subconscious truth serum took over yet again just like it had with the rental property representative. Full transparency was the recipe up until now, like they say if it ain't broke don't fix it. I explained about the car chases in detail and the program director stopped what he was doing, put his pen down, and was watching me explain my story. I went on to explain I had done 18 months probation 10 years before my car chase and had successfully completed that probation. He thanked me for my time and honesty and said they were conducting interviews the rest of the week and he would let me know something as soon as possible.

About 3 weeks had gone by now and it was mid September. I had just enough money left after paying all the expenses since my release to pay October's rent and that was it. I kept submitting applications and working my part-time jobs, but it wasn't generating anywhere near enough to support all that I had absorbed. It was on my lunch break while working at The Villages car wash, that I got the call from the program director at GAMSD. He explained to me that my background check had come back and that the charges that had put me on probation 10 years prior to my car chase incident weren't even on my record! I had told him stuff I didn't even need to! But he said given my transparency and complete honesty along with all the other necessary qualifications and a solid interview, I was offered a position at GAMSD starting at $38,000! I'll never forget the feeling of complete elation, relief, and gratitude. After I hung up I began walking back to the car thinking I guess I don't need this car wash job anymore!

As I reflect on the title of this chapter, The Good Shepherd, it has a threefold meaning. First, how I felt it necessary to reconnect with my son, attempt to be a father again, and be a leader in his life- a Shepherd if you will. Secondly, the irony of a German Shepherd being the vessel that was going to give me an opportunity to support a new life with my son, cannot be overlooked. Third, God was the Good Shepherd and provided me with all the tools along the way to help me with my transition. Think about it:

1. Not being killed justifiably by two separate officers the night of my arrest 10 years ago.

2. The Florida Department of Corrections has 143 facilities. I just happen to be sent to the one that had a dog program tailored for helping veterans?

3. I had the exact amount of money coming out of the work release needed before Guardian Angels hired me.

4. A real estate representative being put in my path with a brother who happened to have a background. This created an emotional connection for my application to be approved.

5. God showed up at the exact moment I needed Him while I'm frozen with anxiety in my car revealing a scripture to bring it all together.

In closing, another observation I want to point out. To those of us with background issues I want something to be made abundantly clear. I was honest with every person, every step of the way about my past. Look people in the eye, take responsibility and there will be a palpable energy that will convey how genuine and sincere you are.

Another piece of advice, get in front of the person who will be making the decision. In my case the rental property representative worked for a Property Management company - typically not a great option for us felons as the application will usually be rejected by a corporation. I had no idea at the time that although the rental representative was Property Management, it was owned by her family. You just never know who you're talking to but being honest made the emotional connection with her and she went to bat for me because of it.

As far as GAMSD, because it was a non-profit there was no corporate machine to go through. Nonprofits by law must have a board of directors but rarely if ever are they involved in the hiring process. I got in front of the decision maker yet again and stayed honest.

The insight I've just shared has come with the luxury of being able to reflect after the fact. If you have the option , take advantage of the information and utilize it for yourself. I can only share with you what worked for me. I'm showing you now the kindness of God and Him being the Good Shepherd and what that's looked like in my life. The sequence of events is beautiful in the way they unfolded, they have God written all over it! It did require me to show up in my own life, be genuine, and trust by faith that God Will Make A Way. God will flex when we demonstrate faith.

Hebrews 11;1
Now Faith is the assurance of things hoped for the evidence of things not seen.

Chapter 6

BEING A CONDUIT

The property at GAMSD was truly something to behold. Its farm-like setting is nestled beautifully in the charming town of Williston Florida in Levy county. It sits on roughly 20 acres of land and has a long driveway ending in a cul-de-sac with a unique octagon-shaped, two-story home that served as headquarters. Corporations as well as wealthy individuals could sponsor a German Shepherd at $25,000 per dog. That sponsorship was used as a tax write-off combined with great public relations for supporting the cause of helping our veterans. Truly brilliant in its simplicity and no doubt a wonderful, noble, and needed service was being provided.

At any given time there are 80-100 German shepherds on the property at various stages of development and training. As I began my new job I was very comfortable in my training ability and working with dogs. Conversely, I was very unsure of my abilities as it pertained to taking a service dog from start to finish. When I was hired it was explained to me that each dog went through six stages prior to being eligible for pairing. Each stage consisted of specific requirements being met in order for the dog to advance to the next stage. Based on my skill set, I was a stage 4 trainer which meant I was getting dogs roughly 6 months old and had them until they were approximately one year old. If a specific task such as seizure response, mobility training, or diabetic alert was needed, the dog would be passed on to stages 5 and 6. However, it was quite common for dogs to be paired after my stage.

As a stage 4 trainer, my responsibilities were to assure the dogs were solid in the basic obedience commands and walking on their leashes properly. Additionally, my stage required me to have all dogs in my inventory pass a Canine good Citizen (CGC) test. The CGC test is a certification program that evaluates a dog's obedience and manners in everyday situations. I would begin introducing things like timed sit stays, downstays, and utilizing both verbal commands and hand signals. All of these types of training exercises were my comfort zone and strengths.

What became a much different and new concept for me is these were going to become service dogs. This meant they were going to have to be exposed and desensitized to all sorts of external stimuli. Everything first starts on campus before they go out in public. I slowly began introducing everyday items they would encounter like: shopping carts, motorized scooters, umbrellas, walkers, and canes. Further challenges existed like introductions to other animals like horses, cows, ducks, and cats all of which resided on the property.

Public Access and "proofing" the service dogs tasks were key responsibilities to my job. Keep in mind, legally a service dog is a service dog because it performs a task. That task must be directly related to the individual's disability. For example, GAMSD dogs knew a minimum of three tasks: 1. Brace-for stability or counterbalance issues. 2. Shield-the dog will stand in any location around the handler providing a barrier between the handler and another person. 3. Paws-the dog will put its front two paws on an elevated surface allowing the recipient to put on the service dog vest. Additionally, this task helps mitigate anxiety and panic attacks by the dog placing its weight on an individual's thighs or chest. Scientific data indicates when a dog performs this task, an individual's heart rate and blood pressure will be reduced. All of our recipients had severe anxiety and all of these tasks became the foundation of my job duties.

As far as public access goes, almost everyday I was out and about exposing dogs to everything possible. This consisted of convenience stores, Wal-Mart, pet stores, elevators, steps, restaurants, malls, airports, Street traffic, public transportation, and having them walk on different textured surfaces. Once I thought a dog was ready to be completed our head trainer would observe me and my dog in public and conduct a public access test. Additionally, the head trainer would observe a cgc test, and ensure that all three tasks were solid on the dog and met the necessary standards and requirements. Once these boxes were checked, my dogs would be ready for pairing unless they needed stages five or six.

During the 10-day pairing process, recipients are introduced to their service dog for the first time. GAMSD provided new recipients with all airfare, car rental cost, and hotel accommodations that are needed. As you can imagine all the veterans coming to us were truly broken people in every way possible. People with severe PTSD, and TBI's (traumatic brain injuries) were the clients I would be interacting with over the pairing process. As part of my training, I had to become PTSD certified. Ironically, during this process it became clear to me I had many of the symptoms myself. A typical list may include: nightmares, avoidance, heightened reactions, anxiety, unwanted memories of trauma, irritability, being triggered by loud noises, substance abuse, sleep issues. As a result, it led me to seek mental health counseling to be diagnosed and in fact confirmed, yes, I also have PTSD.

The pairings are so special. The recipient hasn't been shown a photo or given any details about the dog they are about to be united with. The pairing undoubtedly has a pageantry and ceremonial feel to it. We would have the service dogs hidden out of sight in a horse barn until the moment came to bring them out. As we came out of the horse barn, we walked halfway around the circular driveway as we approached the recipient already seated in a folding chair. We hand the dog off to its new owner as photos and videos of this moment are captured for both sponsors and recipients. The moment is nothing short of pure magic and elation. Every time I walked a dog out I could feel God and it's the only time in my life I felt complete fulfillment.

Each day of the pairing consisted of what we called "turning up the pressure" as gradually the dog and recipient acclimated to one another. The first day for example consisted of the initial introduction and briefly going over some basic commands. Then, strict orders to go back to their hotel and be on a self-imposed house arrest for the night. This creates intense bonding between the dog and the recipient. As the days moved on we went to restaurants, grocery stores, and even partnered with the Gainesville airport TSA for a mock checkpoint scenario.

By the beginning of 2019 I had now been part of several pairings and had helped numerous dogs complete their training. Everyday I was connected to knowing I was helping make an impact on someone's life who desperately needed it. I had never felt more on top of my game and my contributions in life were at an all-time high. I had the privilege of being a conduit between a dog and a human, restoring lives. I couldn't believe my job was this rewarding and fulfilling. I offered to do anything to help our organization including feeding the dogs, taking photos for sponsors, clean company vehicles you name it.

In May of 2019, our head trainer position became available. I was shocked and amazed when our program director asked me if I wanted the promotion and a raise. What I didn't know is that my fellow trainers had asked for me to fill the role. It was so flattering to be thought of so highly by my peers and the organization.

I would like to acknowledge a phenomenal quote from my current counselor and brother in Christ, Dr Vincent Henderson. In one of his four books "Why Didn't Daddy Fix Me?", it perfectly summarizes what God was teaching me: "service is the way to promotion." All of my God-given talent and energy had been put into this job and it didn't seem accurate to refer to this as work- it was service. God had put me in a position to rebuild and restore broken people just like I had been myself.

I'll never forget one woman in particular I had the honor of assisting through a pairing. For the sake of her privacy I'll call her Mary. Mary hadn't left her home in nearly 3 years prior to her arrival due to having been the victim of a sexual assault. When I first met Mary her body language was one of complete despondency and avoidance. Her arms were wrapped tightly around her body as if she couldn't bear the situation and she could barely make eye contact. Her anxiety was constantly on high alert and a panic attack always seemed imminent.

My opening introduction to Mary was something I had never done up until this point. I've learned though when God puts something on your heart, using the Holy Spirit as the conduit, we are just the vessel. I approached Mary and asked her "Do you believe in God?" She looked up at me as tears began to fill her eyes and she said "I used to." I continued to look at her and asked her "Can we pray together?" She immediately reached for my hand and squeezed it, I thought she might break it! I asked God to reveal himself to her during the next 10 days and let Mary know he was there for her. After the prayer she hugged me and we were nearly inseparable during our training sessions. To gain the immediate trust of Mary this quickly was the beauty and Power of God being demonstrated.

On day three of the pairing it is required for the recipients and the dog to be observed in a public setting. Our destination was a Winn-Dixie grocery store. It is totally predictable that at any given point something may trigger a recipient during the pairing. As Mary got out of her vehicle she froze. She cried out to me, "SAM!" Once I got to her she squeezed my hand and said "I can't go in there." This was a common fear of many recipients, simply being out in public can be a huge trigger for those who have PTSD and anxiety. In Mary's case it was extreme, keep in mind she hadn't left her home in almost 3 years let alone go to a grocery store. She had all her groceries delivered to fill those needs up to this point.

This is where my job became crucial because I had an obligation to ensure the dog and recipient were functioning properly. There was never a guarantee that every recipient and every dog were going to work and I was on the front line to be the one approving this. It's a slippery slope to know when I had to push someone through an issue or soften and acquiesce to the moment.

I asked Mary "What is your biggest fear about going in the store?" Her hand tightened even more as I asked the question, she replied "Someone coming up behind me without me knowing." She looked at me and said "Sam, my attacker raped me from behind, I never saw him coming." Mary was revealing the most vulnerable moment in her life to me. As I processed this gut-wrenching revelation I assured Mary that the dog had her '6'. A 6 in military vernacular means they've got you covered so the enemy can't come up behind you. Simply put, it means they've got your back and is a symbol of extreme loyalty.

Remember, one of the service dogs tasks is shield. Reminding Mary of this was very important. I assured Mary no one will ever walk up behind her with a German Shepherd standing behind her. I told her she might as well be walking in the store with a loaded gun - no one will bother her with a 90 pound German Shepherd standing guard. With that understanding, I observed the transformation of this broken woman as her body language became one of confidence and her resolve took root. She put her head up, shoulders back, and walked into and around that store like the terminator. God had given that woman her life back through a dog and allowed me to be a conduit of that process. Several days later that pairing came to a close and Mary and I said our goodbyes. I had never felt more satisfied and I had finally discovered my purpose. Everything in my life felt incredible and I was firing on all cylinders. God was on display everywhere in my life and I felt Him.

After Mary and the other group of recipients departed, I had an appointment to get to. As is common in the industry I had begun taking some training jobs on the side. After my appointment I was traveling north on interstate 75 from Tampa and needed gas. I went inside to grab a snack and a drink. I walked by the alcohol section of the coolers and a Four Loko alcohol beverage just happened to catch my eye. I can remember thinking I've been clean and sober 11 years now, surely enough time has gone by that I can enjoy an alcohol buzz. For reasons still unknown to me I bought two of them. I waited until that evening to drink them knowing I was off the next day to sleep in and relax. I slammed the first one and the feeling of the soothing alcohol began to flood my body. I nursed the second one, watched some tv, enjoyed my buzz, and off to sleep I went. Subconsciously, a seed had been planted in my mind. It convinced me after this brief reintroduction to a world I didn't even realize I missed, that I was perfectly safe- remember Not All Snakes Rattle!

My next week went smoothly at work. At some point shortly before the weekend was about to begin, my mind began anticipating and got excited about being able to enjoy and consume alcohol again. I stopped by the store on my way home and bought a four pack of Four Loko this time. By the end of the third one, I found myself on a prostitution website. The addiction which had been lying dormant, demanded to be fed. I wanted to get high, and where there are prostitutes, there are drugs, plain and simple.

I drove about 30 minutes to Ocala and for the next 3 days relapsed on crack cocaine. I had called into work using sick days, and had texted my son to let him know I was okay but gave a bullshit excuse as to my whereabouts. Once I returned home, I slept, regrouped, and finished out my work week. Having now made a drug connection in Ocala as the next week progressed, my mind was obsessed with having been high. In the recovery world it's referred to as euphoric recall. In my personal experience there is no more addictive substance on the planet than cocaine. My mind was remembering the pleasure of the drug, not the pain after it's all gone. There's a saying "play the tape the whole way through", and remember from past experiences where this will lead. Since the addiction had been fed, it was living in my head rent free, doing push-ups, waiting for the next opportunity. It didn't have to wait long, the very next weekend I was back at it, off to the races.

On the second day of this binge, I had gone through money set aside for my rent. I had also loaned my car out to a drug dealer. My car was later found abandoned on 75 North and the clutch had been completely fried. In less than 2 weeks I went from happily employed, feeling like I was in the presence of God helping people like Mary, to now being without a vehicle, calling into work, and using rent money for drugs. All of this because I thought I could drink successfully again after 11 years of being clean and sober. That's how fast the progressive nature of addiction can be. I now had to admit to my father and son what had happened. Shamefully, not because of anything honest in my intent to own it and learn, but because I was going to need their help to fix what I had just done. My dad cosigned for the home we were in and I spent the rent money. His life's credit is on the line now because of my horrible decisions and selfish behavior.

My son had begun working his first ever job and had a little bit of money. I had put us in a situation where I had to ask my son for money so I could get another car. Without it, there's no way the life we now had would function - I had to get to work it was 60 miles one way. When I called my dad and explained the situation he said " So basically Sam you're asking me to buy your drugs and reimburse you, AND if I don't I screw up my own credit! Not to mention the fact you need more money from Taylor to get a car." He was in the energy between anger, hysteria, and fear of identifying the spot on reality of the situation. He hung up saying "Oh by the way son, how the hell do we know you're not going to do this again next week?!" The only saving grace is there was only one more month before the year lease my dad had co-signed would be over. Far more troubling was my dad knew the strength and unpredictability of my addiction, what had been unleashed, and his grandson was vulnerable to it now.

I managed to stay clean the last month of my lease and didn't miss work. My son loaned me $500 and I used it as a down payment on a 2013 Altima. Taylor had one year left of homeschooling to complete but it was time to completely cut ties with his mom when the lease was up. I had paid Taylor back and secured a rental in Williston just 2 miles away from work through a board member of GAMSD. I'll never forget pulling into a Walmart parking lot with Taylor and letting him know he was going to have to choose whether to come with me or go with his mom. As I reflect on this, he must have been horrified after having seen how quickly I digressed and fell back into an addiction. He really didn't take more than a second to give me his answer when he said "I'm going with you Dad."

What troubles me in retrospect is I appear to have been doing everything right. I was content in life, living my purpose, in a state of fulfillment. There is a spiritual war going on constantly in an invisible world that surrounds us. For the longest time, I never believed the devil was even real. I thought it to be an abstract metaphorical concept of what in psychology they refer to as the shadow. Essentially, it was just us acting out our flawed human defects of character, blaming it on this mystical science fiction like phantom. Perhaps the greatest tool the devil has is our mistaken belief that he's not real. If I were to believe gravity doesn't exist for example, it would quickly be met with the reality of how wrong I was once I take a step off of a 10-story building. My disbelief in gravity no longer has any merit as I would begin to fall to the earth. I believe in the God of the bible- now. At the time I just felt "the presence" of what I understood to be God. The devil didn't want me to enjoy and thrive nor want this book to help you or me and will attack by any means necessary.

John 10:10

10 The thief comes only to steal and kill and destroy; I have come that they may have life, and have it to the full.

Chapter 7

THE THORN IN MY SIDE

During the first few months after the move to Williston, I maintained my job and felt like I was getting back into the swing of life again. Pairings were happening with normal regularity and it was great just having Taylor and I in our own place. The other good thing about the move is it didn't disturb Taylor's school as he continued to be enrolled online for his senior year and found a job in town.

As the holidays were rolling around an issue at work was developing. A training technique known as early neurological stimulation (ENS), was used on all new litters of puppies. ENS is a series of gentle exercises that are performed on puppies during a critical period of their development. The goal of ENS is to improve a puppy's neurological development, learning capacity, and ability to cope with stress. ENS is performed daily from the third to the 16th day of a puppy's life. It involves applying gentle stressors, such as tactile stimulation, thermal stimulation, and holding the puppy in different positions for a few seconds. The U.S. military used ENS in the 1970s to produce "superdogs" that were better able to detect threats.

The downside to this technique is if it's not done properly it can have permanent long term effects on the dogs confidence or in the industry what we called "nerve". Dogs can appear skiddish or overly distracted and it can take considerably longer to train them and in many cases the dogs can't overcome the issue. All of the trainers began coming to me with concerns of numerous dogs having issues in public. Specifically, an inability to have the confidence or nerve in public that would be required. An example would be as you approach any automatic sliding doors to enter a building. As the doors would open, the dogs would seem extremely startled and had their head on a swivel. An unexpected object or external stimuli may cause the dog to become startled and a reaction is expected. As trainers we looked for the dog to recover. Simply put, after a few seconds, whatever initially startled them should no longer be a factor. We were in the business of providing service dogs and any dog we provided for the veterans couldn't under any circumstances be hindered by this kind of limitation.

As these issues progressed, we began to put together that it was all the same litter of dogs that was having the issue. Further investigation uncovered that the common denominator is that their ENS had not been done properly. I was the liaison between what was going on with the training of our dogs and the administrative staff that ran the sponsorship side of our organization. I had the dubious obligation of having to inform our CEO and COO that we had 12 dogs that in our professional opinion were not going to be able to make it as service dogs.

At a sponsorship price tag of $25,000 per dog, that's a $300,000 cost to the organization, or said another way, revenue that couldn't be earned. Not to mention additional costs the organization spent on medical care, food, and what the organization was spending on payroll for us as trainers this whole time. It also put the sponsorship team in the uncomfortable situation of now having to approach sponsors, explain the situation, and ask for their continued support and patience. The decision was made to put a halt on all pairings for the next several months until the next group of dogs would be ready. This would take us into the first quarter of 2020 before any pairings would be possible.

There are a handful of historical events that are markers in my lifetime. My earliest sports memory, for example, was the 1980 U.S. men's Olympic hockey team winning the gold medal. I remember the assassination attempt on Ronald Reagan, the explosion of the space shuttle Challenger in the mid-1980s, the tearing down of The Berlin Wall, the crumbling of The Soviet Union, and of course 9/11. However, what was about to have the largest impact on my life was the covid-19 pandemic. In March of 2020 our entire country began to notice something astronomically huge was on the horizon.

To this day, it's impossible to quantify the impact covid-19 had on not just our country, but the world as a whole. Everything from our economy, schools, ability to travel, restaurants, our country was on a lockdown. As a result, depression, suicides, anxiety, drug and alcohol abuse we're at an all-time high, truly we were in unprecedented times. As far as the immediate impact on my life, I had now gone 5 full months without having had a pairing when the lockdown came. Our organization gave the entire staff a one-month furlough and we would then touch base to determine the next course of action. GAMSD was a non-profit organization so it was driven almost exclusively by donations. When the pandemic hit, people were terrified of what was going to happen with their money. Donations dried up quickly and organizations like ours took a huge hit financially. When the 1 month furlough had elapsed, the organization was unable to bring the majority of the staff back at nothing more than minimum wage.

Given the totality of the situation, I thought my best choice was to go on unemployment and end my time at GAMSD. If there was a decision I could go back and undo, I feel it would be this one. At the time, the federal government was giving a $600 weekly boost to any state's unemployment. Florida, had one of the lowest weekly payouts at $275 however, it was going to be generating me $875 a week with the extra assistance from the government for at least the next 6 months. My monthly expenses were no more than $1,300 a month. So if you do the math, I was generating $3,500 a month, with only $1300 in expenses. That's giving me a little over $2,000 a month free and clear to play with and nothing but idle time.

I was once again disconnected from helping people, living my purpose, and serving others. One industry that benefited from the shutdown was drug dealing. Additionally, prostitution seemed to be booming as well. I began seeking other areas besides Ocala to explore. I began networking and hanging out with multiple women in different locations and hotels. My spending was careless, extreme, and of course the fact I was spending $1000-$2000 every time I showed up, provided me with immediate popularity amongst the women and dealers.

There wasn't any shortage of "friends" and you could easily see the jealousy amongst the different women lobbying for my time. I want to again keep anonymity, however there was one girl in particular I used to hang out with. She was in a hotel, it was always safe, and no questions were asked. It became almost like a little hideout for me. Various dealers were aware when I was in town and it wasn't uncommon that we would make runs to pick up our dope. My point is, I was becoming a known name in that area's drug underworld.

As the Federal weekly supplement of $600 came to an end, it became necessary to find employment. While I was on this hiatus, I was able to drum up additional dog training business in The Villages. One particular dog park allowed me to do weekend training for CGC testing. This created additional revenue streams as many of my clients wanted me to do personal training with their dogs as well.

I eventually saw an ad for a dog training company that's hiring trainers to do training from their own home. This was a UK based company that was expanding into the United States. Florida was one of the first States they were expanding into, and they needed trainers quickly. They had a sales and marketing team that would be securing the dogs that needed training. All of their marketing data indicated Florida was fertile ground to generate some serious revenue. Just to give you an idea, I would go and pick the dog up and drop the dog off after training was completed. The company charged $2,000 for 2 weeks, $3,000 for 3 weeks, and $4,000 for 4 weeks.

I was hired at $60,000 a year as well as being paid .75 cents per mile to pick up and drop off every dog I needed to train. Additionally, I was going to be paid $14 for every hour I spent on the road. It was common for me to travel from Williston to places like Tampa, Orlando, and as far south as Fort Lauderdale or Miami. We're talking several hundred miles round trip and my pick up and drop off days sometimes consisted of 16 to 18 hour days. I was easily earning in the ballpark of $8000 a month, and my expenses still weren't exceeding $1,300 a month.

I began timing my pickups and drop offs of the dogs around my ability to get high. Now, I had even more money to spend and was deep in the throes of active addiction. It was during this time that fentanyl started becoming popular in and around the circle of people I was with. Personally, I had no desire to use it, but no doubt it was becoming prevalent. Sadly, I got a phone call informing me that my female friend I hung out with in the hotel,had died from a fentanyl overdose. She had been my go-between when it came to scoring dope. I never minded having an individual between me and the buy, after having done 10 years in prison. It was the cost of doing business. Nothing however keeps the addiction train from moving. All the dealers knew me and now I had direct access. Quickly we developed a comfort level with one another and I began using a lot of different locations within the area and scoring from multiple dealers. There was no shortage of where to go, or women to hang out with because everyone knew how much money I was spending. I guess it was the closest thing to Rockstar status I could have obtained.

When I would come back home and get back to work with the dogs, I knew I was losing control of my life. My timing was off, my tolerance was very thin, and my mind was completely obsessed with figuring out when I was going to go get high again. My son had finished high school and was in the process of moving out of state. It seemed only appropriate for him to drive the Altima while I would follow by driving his car out to his new home a few days later. I figured if anything went wrong with his car at least I would be in a position to pay for it. In hindsight, I should have just given Taylor the Altima. These are things now that I'm clean and clear headed that make obvious sense. The drive was several states away and I can remember thinking I knew I was completely out of control but told myself at least I had not ever put a needle in my arm- yet.

I had been promoted to the head trainer position of the new company that I was working for. I conducted weekly meetings through Zoom, and trainers from Florida all the way up the East Coast reported back to me. During this time I was feeling desperate for something positive. God had put it on my heart to go back to the prison I had been released from, Tomoka Correctional. As I pondered the implications the answer seemed to feel right at the time, to be part of a dog graduation. It would serve a dual purpose. First, to be able to explain to the guys I had become The head trainer of a global dog training organization. This would help them know and be encouraged that what they were doing now actually can pay dividends - I was once them. Second, maybe seeing the prison again would be a reminder that this is where I may be headed if I don't stop. I called classification at the prison, got cleared, and in a few months was scheduled to be the guest speaker for the upcoming dog graduation.

As caught up in the addiction as I was, I would maintain 3 weeks out of the month to ensure I was training dogs and generating revenue. This was also in large part because we were only paid once a month so when I got paid, I partied. There was an issue with our paychecks in spring of 2022, specifically, we never got one. We all received an email ensuring it was a "glitch." Something to do with the UK banking system the company used converting Bitcoin to the British pound and then to US dollars. I was being told this info by text from the COO of the company. I was flooded nonstop with phone calls and texts by my trainers demanding answers and paychecks.

I was told the issue was being worked on and we had nothing to worry about. I looked people in their eyes on Zoom meetings and did my best damage control going to bat for the company. All of my trainers including myself were at capacity with dogs working on good faith. My team believed what I was telling them in large part because I'm an effective communicator and salesman. I then received a call from the South American branch of our company informing me all the company's bank accounts had been frozen. The CEO of our company had disappeared, now sought for questioning by Interpol, leaving 125 people in 6 different countries, without pay.

To process what just happened had my head spinning. My skill set of being an effective communicator had been used to manipulate employees that trusted me. The only revenue I had was a tax refund I was waiting on to come in. My landlord informed me when my lease was up in a month, she was not giving me the option to renew. It wasn't that I had done anything wrong, but she was ready to turn the house into an Airbnb. I was going to be left with nowhere to live, no job, and no way to pay for my car. I had no savings, because every penny had been spent towards feeding the addiction and the lifestyle that went along with it. Addiction hadn't been my problem, it was my solution. It was a coping mechanism, my escape, my excuse, and physiologically my brain had been rewired due to my own reinforcement of the behavior.

I want to be as perfectly clear, honest, and direct as I possibly can be. Me, and me alone, are responsible for my choices and consequences. That being said, the pandemic hitting when it did was horrible timing for my life. No doubt this was the case for many people. However, I felt like I was just getting back into the swing of life again and being connected to serving my purpose when we went on lockdown. Everything else that happened after that is a snowball effect of allowing myself to get caught back up in active addiction.

The addiction is the thorn in my side. Out of desperation and an attempt to neutralize the addiction, I begged God to remove it. To date, it has not been removed. I was angry and confused as to why God would allow such a destructive thorn to remain? God's silence was deafening. How could a loving God turn his back on His own child, crying out for help? I would like to point out Paul's scripture on this topic:

2 Corinthians 12: 7-10

A thorn was given me in the flesh. Three times I appealed to the Lord about this, that it would leave me but he said to me "my grace is sufficient for you, for power is made perfect in my weakness." So I will boast all the more gladly of my weaknesses, so that the power of Christ may dwell in me. Therefore, I am content with weaknesses for whenever I am weak then I am strong.

It is only after having time to reflect and do some deep introspection while in rehab, that I'm able to provide myself and hopefully anyone who reads this with some answers. I didn't know this then. At the time I was so confused, hopeless, and shattered. I'm giving you my realizations and discoveries now, 5 years later, so that perhaps you may gain some clarity and understanding if you feel like God has abandoned you or deserted you. In these moments of crisis and trials, there are going to be times God won't remove the issue. It doesn't mean he's not there but rather trusts you with that particular trial. What I've learned, and submitted to you, is I can be grateful for the thorn in my side. It forces me to go to God everyday, so that I stay connected to the vine and where I am weak He is strong.

The writing of the last 2 chapters has been extremely challenging. It's been revealed to me just how stuck and trapped I've been in a self defeating energy of shame and guilt the last 5 years. I have had intense drug dreams. In those dreams I have packed a stem, hit it, as I watched the smoke fill the chamber. I have woken up sitting in my bed attempting to blow the hit out.

Conversely, having had this insight, I feel grateful to uncover where I've been stuck. There's no reason, nor does it serve any purpose, to stay in that narrative. My life and your life is in front of us not behind us. We create our momentum by being in line with God's will and serving our purpose. My good friend Nick reminded me of a financial formula that I feel is applicable, "Past performance is no indication of future return."

Phillipians 4:8-9

Finally, brethren, whatsoever things are true, whatsoever things are honest, whatsoever things are just, whatsoever things are pure, whatsoever things are lovely, whatsoever things are of good report; if there be any virtue, and if there be any praise, think on these things. Those things, which ye have both learned, and received, and heard, and seen in me, do: and the God of peace shall be with you.

The next 3 chapters are going to have tremendous contrasts and pendulum swings. I pray God will help me communicate in an effective manner the depths of my despair and my inspirational hope that only He can provide.

Chapter 8

DAILY REPRIEVE

Just as the door on my life in Williston was being slammed shut, I received a job offer training dogs again. It just so happened that it required me to spend 10 days in the Boca Raton area for orientation training. The hotel accommodations were paid for by the company and I timed those 10 days to start with the ending of my lease in Williston. I at least provided myself somewhere to live for the next 10 days and thought, I'll figure it out from there. It was the evening of the 5th day into my orientation when I received a knock on my hotel door. It was one of the dog training company's administrative staff handing me a copy of my background. I was never told one was being conducted or I would have headed this off at the pass as I have before. I had been so disconnected from life that I violated my own rule, be transparent. In any event, I was told I had an hour to gather my belongings and get out, my job offer had been rescinded.

I had some per diem money left and there was a 7-11 right down the road from the hotel. All I remember thinking is, "I bet if I sat in that parking lot long enough, I'll find someone to sell me dope." I went inside the store, bought a 6 pk of something, and began pounding beers. I had my car backed into a parking spot with the driver side window down. Having been all too familiar with this lifestyle combined with having some liquid courage in me, I began surveilling the scene looking for a likely supplier. It didn't take long before a prolonged stare from someone at a gas pump warranted the approach. I bought some crack and was given a phone number. That fast a connection had been made. I had enough money to keep me on a decent binge, combined with what was always a backup revenue/dope payment- being a driver.

I had been up for 2 days going on 3, when my Google calendar gave me a 24 hour notice that I was due to speak at Tomoka for the dog graduation. Again my attention to detail was non-existent. It never crossed my mind that I had scheduled my orientation to conflict with my speaking obligation at Tomoka. I don't know what threw the switch but I felt as if somehow my life depended on getting there. I made a last run for my new business partner and split my last payment: half money, half dope.

By the time I headed north on 95 from Boca Raton, I had about 8 hours to get to Tomoka in Daytona Beach. It was roughly a 3 1/2 hr drive. I got out of Boca Raton as fast as possible and waited to hit my dope so I wouldn't consider turning around. I stopped to pick up some toiletries, get gas, and keep it moving.

I was about an hour away from Tomoka and now out of dope. I was abruptly startled by my passenger window being shattered and my windshield spider- webbing in all directions. I had fallen asleep behind the wheel and veered into another lane, sideswiping a Charger. It was autopilot to pull over on the shoulder and process what had happened. The other driver got out, as did I. He was in his 20's and appeared far more anxious than I was. He looked at me and said "sir, I have pot in the car, do we have to call the police?" I probably looked like The Cheshire Cat, and calmly replied "no young man, we don't."

To say I had dodged a bullet in every possible way is an understatement. I could have seriously hurt or killed someone, not to mention myself. I hadn't even been injured. I had paraphernalia in my car and if the cops had been called, which would have normally been the case, I would have been arrested. As the driver of the freshly sideswiped Charger drove off, I cleaned my car out putting all drug related items into a bag and walked it out into the woods off the Interstate for discarding. What was I thinking anyway? I wasn't far from pulling into a prison parking lot where drug dogs are walking around all visitors' vehicles.

After ridding my vehicle of felony charges, I was back on the road with a seriously damaged vehicle. The windshield alone was grounds to be pulled over but I still had plenty of time to make it to Tomoka. It was about 15 minutes after sideswiping the Charger, that I again was awoken by the sound of crunching metal. This time, I had run into the back of an Altima. As our vehicles pulled off onto the shoulder, amazingly, very minor damage had been done to the front end of my car. Fortunately, they had crossed over into my lane and said they lightly applied their brakes minimizing the impact as I rear-ended them. I had fallen asleep again, and was responsible for two accidents now not even 20 minutes apart.

As a result of this accident the police did get called. When they arrived I acknowledged I had dozed off and preliminary accident protocols began. At no point was there ever any accusations of any kind or a field sobriety test performed. While I waited for the reports to be completed I called my dad. I told him what had happened and I could hear the concern and heartbreak that any parent would have for their child given the totality of my history.

My dad shared the story of a documentary that reminded him of what was going on with my life. The documentary was on mountain climbers. The mountain climbers were interviewed about everything that would involve their climb to the summit. Contingency plans for weather, food rations, where they would camp out for the night, what gear they would need, communications, etc... It took months and months of careful planning before the climb began. All of the individuals interviewed were engaged and enthralled while discussing this part of the expedition.

As the story progressed, all the mountain climbers achieved their goal of reaching the summit. There was celebration and congratulations as the victorious participants took in the scenery and marveled at the view around them. As they discussed their descent however, a look of darkness and depression overtook them. There was the sudden realization that although they had accomplished their goal, it was now over, there was no more mountain to conquer. They were left feeling empty and unfulfilled because there was no plan after the mountain. My dad said to me "son, you need to find another mountain to conquer."

My father was summarizing my life in those years after getting out of prison. I had accomplished the goal of reuniting with my son, gotten a good job, car, home- I had climbed my mountain. Once I got to my summit, looked around and enjoyed the view, I quickly became anxious and saddened. There was nothing left to accomplish and as I began my descent, there wasn't a concept of what now? An all too familiar cyclical pattern of self destruction had emerged as my father in loving desperation said "son, you haven't learned how to handle your freedom."

As I pulled into Tomoka it occurred to me my original reason for coming didn't exist any more. At the time I had scheduled myself to be the guest speaker, I was the head trainer of a global dog training organization. Not only that but I'm showing up homeless, jobless, having just had 2 car accidents, with cocaine in my system. What was I supposed to say? What could

I offer? I was coming to share the ultimate comeback story, and be an example of how to reacclimate to society.

I was being propelled by a force I didn't comprehend and pulled into Tomoka as if by magnet. I was greeted by an officer that immediately recognized me and shook my hand. I was escorted into the dog graduation and handed a program. I looked down at it as if to verify my name was still in it, and took a seat. The room began to fill with people from the VA, prison officials including the warden, and happy new dog owners. After preliminary introductions I was called to the podium.

I was completely unprepared, suddenly overwhelmed, and had no clue what to say as I made my way to the front. As I scanned the crowd, Psalm 46:10 again came into my consciousness "Be Still and Know That I Am God". What was put on my heart to talk about was the story and message my father had just told me while I was on the side of the road. The message couldn't have been more appropriate for this audience. After the story of the mountain climbers, I shared the successes I had upon my release. I was able to compare this to the mountain climbers as they achieved the summit. Conversely, I explained what happened with the pandemic, and most recently a fraudulent business owner that brought me to where I am to share this story with all of you. I closed with expressing my belief in the strength of God and ended by quoting Psalm 46:10- Be still and know that I am God.

When I got done, there wasn't a dry eye in the room, and I received a standing ovation. As I left the podium I just remember there being a sea of hands for me to shake and a few hugs for good measure. Even in this complete debacle of a day, there was some profound deep meaning and purpose God had for getting me to Tomoka that day. I needed to GIVE the message about the mountain as much as the guys in the dog program needed to hear it. I was commended for a brilliant message by dozens of people! What had just happened? I went there completely broken, embarrassed, feeling shame, and thinking I had nothing to offer. My emotions stood in complete juxtaposition to one another, consumed by darkness, as I marveled at the greatness of God.

It was nearly the end of 2022, and I had been as out of control as I had ever been in my life. I was doing local drug runs for dealers, picking up and dropping off prostitutes that somehow had become "friends." Sleep only came as a result of passing out and food was a second thought. During this time period I would periodically call my dad and my son just as a courtesy to let them know I was alive. Everything that I had once felt connected to that was fulfilling and edifying in my life was a distant memory. I was completely consumed by the darkness and demonic energy of addiction, chasing temporary fleeting moments that eroded the very core of my soul hit after hit.

In late December, about 2am, I got pulled over as a result of nodding off and veering sharply onto the shoulder. I was informed my license had been suspended as of midnight that night. I acknowledged I had fallen asleep and was given a citation because the cop took pity on me that I was living out of my car and hadn't received notification from the insurance company. I was lucky because driving on a suspended license in Florida will get you arrested. Not even 2 days later, I was stopped, questioned, and somehow talked my way out of being arrested, again.

At no point during my off and on indulgences into the drug world, will any place compare to The Capital. It was the mecca of all things drug-related. Every possible hedonistic behavior you could conceive of was being satisfied at The Cap. This was the land of overachievers when it came to street life being combined with the party life. Anything from trafficking, manufacturing, prostitution, dealing in stolen property, and pretty much any felonious activity was facilitated at The Cap. It was the ultimate trap house. The Cap had several rooms in it all of which had monitors for surveillance. You could never tell what day of the week it was because the traffic in and out of there was nonstop 24/7. The only thing I've experienced on this level relative to time being so irrelevant is Las Vegas. Various people of different status at some point throughout the day would arrive, hangout, conduct whatever business or service needed rendering and round and round it went.

As I was returning to The Capital after a delivery, I evidently didn't stop properly at a stop sign and was again pulled over. Somehow I talked my way out of being arrested again, but this time the officer physically removed the tag off my car. He allowed me to be followed by a friend of mine who happened to be driving by while I was stopped. I returned to The Capital where I partied well into the next day. At some point, I was asked by a "female friend" if I'd take her to her dad's house to pick up some items and return. I told her my car didn't have a tag to which she said " I don't care if you don't." As dumb as it was, I made the drive. We made it safely to her dad's. However on the way back, we got stopped by the police. My car was impounded, I was arrested for driving on a suspended license, and sentenced to 10 days in jail. As a result of the multiple driving on a suspended license, the State of Florida has revoked my driver's license for 5 years.

After my 10-day time out, I returned to The Capital. I still did some deliveries on bicycle, and continued to stay in active addiction. Things went from bad to worse as I made the decision to shoot up for the first time. I didn't know how to do it myself so I had someone experienced in doing it "hit me." It was meth, which was not my normal drug of choice but the excitement of those around me convinced me it was something I needed to try. Unfortunately, my vein was missed and I wound up having to go to the emergency room as my forearm nearly doubled in size. I was given an IV for a couple hours and right back to the Capital I went. One of the dealers was going to be gone for the night and offered his room to me and I had a supply of cocaine. As was usually the case, I was trusted in and around supply, and money. Just to err on the side of caution the room was locked from the outside with a padlock. Even though I was trusted, there's always a paranoia and vulnerability of supply and money being exposed so it was a safety measure combined with me being perfectly willing to be left alone.

After my supply of cocaine ran out, I was laying on the bed. My eyes began to wander to the floor and over in the corner, underneath the desk, was a big white chunk. To all of us that understand, it's a complete impulse and reaction to go on a reconnaissance mission. I put the piece on the end of my stem, lit it, took a big pull, and the last thought I remember having is "why isn't there any noise?" To those of us that know about crack cocaine, as soon as the flame hits the rock, there is a "crack"ing sound. this wasn't the case, I lost consciousness and fell to the ground. When the paramedics arrived I was dead.

As I have written this chapter and reflect, what comes to my mind is a quote from the Big book of alcoholics anonymous. This quote is not limited to those that identify as an addict or an alcoholic, and in my opinion is a blueprint for life. "What we really have is a daily reprieve contingent on the maintenance of our spiritual condition. Everyday is a day when we must carry the vision of God's will into all of our activities. "How can I best serve Thee - Thy will (not mine) be done." These are thoughts which must go with us constantly. We can exercise our will power along this line all we wish. It is the proper use of the will."

I had been as far away from this wisdom as one could possibly get. My will felt as if it wasn't my own. All of my consequences were the result from the seed of a tree I planted. The scriptures below define the spiritual battle I had exposed myself to.

GALATIANS 5: 16-20

16 So I say, walk by the Spirit, and you will not gratify the desires of the flesh. 17 For the flesh desires what is contrary to the Spirit, and the Spirit what is contrary to the flesh. They are in conflict with each other, so that you are not to do whatever[a] you want. 18 But if you are led by the Spirit, you are not under the law.

19 The acts of the flesh are obvious: sexual immorality, impurity, idolatry, sorcery, strife, jealousy, anger, quarrels, envy, drunkenness, carousing, and things like these.

As always though God gives us the answers if only we would listen:

GALATIANS 5:22-23

By contrast, the fruit of the spirit is love, joy, peace, patience, kindness, generosity, faithfulness, gentleness, and self-control.

What happens next I cannot explain.

Chapter 9

THE VOICE OF GOD

When I regained consciousness, I was in an ambulance. Shouts of "Sam! Sam! Welcome back!" were the first things I heard along with the sound of my heartbeat on the monitor I was hooked to. I will explain to you, what has been explained to me, regarding the events that transpired to get me in that ambulance. I will then give an account of my experience and recollection of my death and the closest thing I can hope to share with you regarding the voice of God and my connection to Him.

First, what I put on my stem and hit wasn't crack, but fentanyl. A person in the next room heard a "thump", which was me hitting the floor. Something told her that sounded odd, she came to investigate, and began hollering my name through the padlocked door. I didn't give a response which gained the attention of another person. Together, they hollered as I remained silent, and frantically began trying to knock on the door. Now, in a complete panic, they began trying to bust the door open but couldn't. It was at this point a friend had enough strength and adrenaline to literally kick the door off the hinges. I was laying on the floor, unconscious, and my lips had already begun turning blue. The fact that 911 was called is a miracle given what went on at The Capital. It's a testimony that although all of our lives at The Cap were dysfunctional and toxic, at least there was a call for help. I owe my deepest gratitude.

I was told by EMS personnel that it was approximately 20 minutes before the paramedics got to me. What I do know, is I was later informed by paramedics I was dead on arrival (DOA). I was told that 4 Narcan containers were used while CPR was being performed. There was no response as I was put into the ambulance. During the time I was unresponsive, I experienced the most peaceful, loving energy and felt as though I was entering an expansion of sorts. I wasn't thinking anything, but knowing I was in a place of safety, home if you will.. I can't say I saw anything, only felt what I've described. I'm attempting to explain the unexplainable. At some point an audible question entered my awareness and consciousness that asked "Do you want to go back?" As soon as whatever part of "me" acknowledged "yes", I was brought back into the realm of our current reality.

As the ambulance continued its way to the hospital I flatlined. My consciousness and awareness never faded, never dimmed, and at no point can I say I didn't know exactly what was going on. Shouts from the paramedics screaming "we've lost him, no vitals", echoed through the ambulance. I HEARD everything, I SAW nothing. There was no concept of time but the same energy that was present before again asked " Do you want to go back?" I wasn't scared or concerned, and was completely at peace. Whatever part of my existence was communicating with this energy again responded "yes", and I was catapulted back into the realm of the living.

"What just happened to me?", I asked the paramedics. " You flatlined Sam, you died" was the response. I was encouraged to talk, say the ABC's, count, anything to stay with them. I explained what I experienced and there was a look of both curiosity and an unknowing of how to respond from the paramedics. All they could tell me is that I was dead when they first got to me, and I had died on them again on the way to the hospital. It will take the rest of my life to process what I experienced.

Only a month or so had passed since my overdose and near-death experience (NDE). Unfortunately, despite being allowed to live, I returned to active addiction. Just before sunrise on the morning of April 27th 2023, I had gotten a 50 piece of crack cocaine. I hopped on my bike and began heading to The Cap a few miles away. I had just gotten to the top of a hill and was coasting a bit to get my wind before the descent on the other side. I was almost at full speed and beginning to catch the downside of the hill when a Jeep doing nearly 55 MPH ran into me from behind. I got absolutely crushed.

Eyewitness testimony described me as being "windmilled" through the air as my head hit the guardrail on the side of the road, splitting it open at both temples, fracturing numerous ribs, and breaking the L1 in my back. I remember somehow getting to my feet as passengers from cars that had stopped began screaming for me to lay down. The looks on their faces easily told the horror of what had just happened. As I put my hands to my head and pulled them down to look, they were covered in blood and I began to go into shock. As the pain all over my body began to announce its presence, I was having my hand held by a complete stranger and assured the ambulance was on its way.

I remember hearing the sound of the sirens getting nearer as I stared at the sky begging God not to let me die. The first officer on the scene, ironically, is the one who had put me in jail and impounded my car just a few months prior. Once the ambulance arrived, I heard him holler out my name to the paramedics. The paramedics began shouting "we need the helicopter or he's not gonna make it!" The response from dispatch was that they had none available. The reality of what I had just heard from dispatch told me this is how I'm gonna die. I continued staring at the sky, crying, waiting to die, as I slipped into a blackened void. I found out later, the police investigation had turned the case over to vehicular homicide as they were certain I was not going to make it.

Paramedics later told me blood pressure and pulse showed no signs of activity, "for some time" as CPR was administered. My next memory was someone shouting "Sam, do you want to live!?" "Sam, do you want to live!?" I looked up and the female paramedic was staring right into my soul. I said "Yes, please don't let me die." I stared back up at the sky and said "God, what do you want from me?" The paramedic answered as if she knew and replied "Be Still and Know That I Am God. God's got you Sam."

After being released from the ER, I went to stay with my cousin in Maryland to heal. After 2 months, I decided to return to Florida. Within a month of my return I had been arrested for possession of cocaine. My dad bonded me out, and 2 months later I was arrested again for possession which revoked my bond. As a result, I would spend the next 10 months in jail. My county jail issued tablets to all inmates. One of the apps on the tablet is called PANDO. The following is taken directly off of the internet describing what PANDO is:

Our free app delivers content like sermons, worship music, devotionals, podcasts, and other spiritual growth content directly into the hands of incarcerated people all over the country. Pando is the very first app of its kind available to people who are incarcerated. Pando makes it possible for inmates all over the country to experience Christ's love through life-changing content, 24/7, through a secure app on their provided tablets.

It was during these 10 months God revealed Himself to me more and more. Out of sheer boredom I began watching The Chosen and sermons from several different churches on my tablet. I've never doubted an intelligent design that made our universe and the world in which we live. So, I began to ask myself what would God's purpose be in creation? The Chosen did an incredible job at showing me the relational aspect of Jesus' nature. In so doing, it seemed reasonable to be open to the possibility God wants a relationship with me. With willingness came an increased capacity. It dawned on me that perhaps my questions and doubts about Christianity needed to be revisited.

A major turning point in my journey was about to reveal itself to me. I had always known my name Samuel was biblical in its origin, however I had no familiarity with the story or its significance. Little did I know that Samuel heard the voice of God. To be sitting in jail processing what was unfolding as I read the story of Samuel, it was as if God was announcing His presence once again.

In the Bible, Samuel heard the voice of God in 1 Samuel 3 while he was sleeping in the temple. Samuel thought the voice was the priest Eli, but it was actually God calling him to be a prophet.

What happened?
Samuel heard a voice calling his name

Samuel thought it was Eli, so he called back, "Here I am"

Eli was asleep, so he didn't respond

Samuel ran to Eli, woke him, and said, "Here I am"

Eli said he didn't call Samuel and sent Samuel back to bed

This happened two more times that night

On the third time, Eli realized that it was God calling Samuel

What did Eli teach Samuel?

Eli taught Samuel to say, "Speak, Lord, for your servant is listening". Samuel went back to bed and God called him again, and Samuel said, "Speak, Lord, for your servant is listening".

What did this story teach me?

For me, it's incredibly personal, which by the way shows the relational aspect of God's nature with us as his creation. This story shows that God speaks to people and how he has revealed himself to me. Another point I'd like to make is Samuel's response in the Bible when he first hears the voice of God. "Here I Am." It reminded me of psalm 46:10 " be still and know that I AM God." Keep in mind that verse has been inserted several different times in my life. The significance for me is that prior to my conversion to Christianity, I took that verse and the "I Am" part very differently, and as a result had a misguided trajectory of its meaning. The books I had been reading in prison in hindsight were all a self deification process by cultivating The Great "I Am." Yes we all have a piece of God in us, but it is impossible for us to be our own God.

God was connecting dots for me so obvious, they can't be argued. My name is Samuel , and yes, I unequivocally believe I too, have heard the voice of God. What else asked me when confirmed dead by medical personnel "Do you want to go back?" It is beyond obvious God has been sending me a message to share what has happened to me. It's not really even my story, but God revealing Himself through me.

My prior beliefs going back to the books I shared I had been reading in prison, all discussed developing a greater version of myself by elevating awareness to achieve higher states of enlightenment. What I discovered as I was sitting in jail yet again, is how obvious it is I have a problem with authority. My obstacle with Christianity was its exclusive claim that it had a monopoly on God. Was Jesus really saying he was the only way to God? Is the bible really the inspired word of God? How can it be if it's written by man? Aren't these ancient texts just copies of copies? And perhaps the largest obstacle that remained in my mind, what about this alleged Resurrection?

Matthew 7:7-8 says, "Ask, and it will be given to you; seek, and you will find; knock, and the door will be opened to you".

As someone who has experienced something as surreal as having my life given back to me, I have spent countless hours watching any type of videos and gaining knowledge on the topic of near death experiences (NDE). It has also led me on a journey of spiritual discovery, faith, and why I have come to believe in the God of the Bible. I mentioned in my introduction to this book that I was the biggest cynic as it pertained to the Bible that I had ever met. Moving forward, I'm going to ask that you trust I have done my due diligence into the research that I'm about to discuss. It will be broken down into 3 parts: Proof of God, The Bible, The Resurrection. All of these topics could take up an entire book by themselves. I have been on a search for truth all my life and this is what I've discovered. My journey to the discovery of what I have been sharing with you throughout this book, is coming to a head.

Chapter 10

PROOF OF GOD

Came To Believe (Part 1)

Of the three categories I'm about to discuss, this one has never been in question. However to connect the stream of thought from God, to the Bible, to the resurrection, it's necessary to have some foundational starting points. One of the biggest misconceptions I had is that science stood in opposition to God. I have come across documentaries, YouTube videos, books, and conversations in which there would be accredited scientists, many of whom were atheists, discussing their arguments against intelligent design. I've never doubted the existence of God, but maybe you have been uncertain or unconvinced and I can show you what I've learned after countless hours of research which I believe to be the best evidence or "proof." I have a lot of passion about this topic and while God doesn't boast, I marvel at his design. When it comes to knowing there is a God, it's game, set, match.

For those of you who are incarcerated go on your PANDO app, then 121 Community Church app. Scroll down until you see the category "lenses," and then click on "faith + science." For those who have internet access, go on YouTube and search Dr. James Tour. He is a synthetic organic chemist from Rice University, and look for his " origin of life" teaching lesson. He will show you the origin of life like it is taught in any classroom, school or university as it pertains to the complexity of a cell purely from a scientific standpoint. The results will be obvious, this is the origin of life aka, (OOL).

In his presentation the question is posed "What is the origin of life?" "It's a cell that is an amazing machine, not a blob from some primordial soup. A cell is a factory. It has the lipid bi-layer which allows and rejects what is allowed into it. A cell has areas where energy is produced, microtubules which move matter from point A to point B. You can visually picture this yourself by thinking of any factory you've seen. It has the ability to transfer materials in a specific, sequential, chronological order for maximum efficiency. After the microtubule breaks down, it regenerates and has the capability of self-replication and moves to somewhere else. If you want an origin of life discussion this is where you start. No one has ever done this in a lab and if you've been taught or read this, you've been lied to." The assertion was quite clear; If a cell could be manufactured in a lab, God was out of a job.

"Why do textbooks then say that OOL has been replicated in a lab?" "Every chemical synthesis experiment in origin of Life research looks like this:

• They purchase some chemicals in high purity from a chemical company
• They mix those chemicals together in water and high concentration in a specific order under some set of carefully devised conditions in a lab
• Obtain a mixture of compounds that have a resemblance to one or more of the four classes of chemicals needed for life: carbohydrates, nucleic acid, amino acid and lipids
• Then they publish a paper making bold assertions about the origin of life from these functionless crude mixtures. This was done by Miller in 1952.
• Engage with the ever gullible press to exert their alleged findings

- An uninformed lay person now asserts "scientists understand how life formed"
- Lastly, encourage a generation of science textbook writers to make colorful deceptive cartoons of raw chemicals assembling cells which then emerge as slithering creatures from a prehistoric pond."

As I continued looking for any type of scientific proof of God, what occurred to me, is I was attempting to use my finite human mind to explain that which is infinite. Albert Einstein's original theory is that the universe always existed thus eliminating the first cause, therefore removing God as that first cause. It wasn't until Edwin Hubble convinced Einstein that he must change his findings, why? It was revealed that the universe is both expanding and accelerating thus proving it had an origin. This led Einstein to reverse his hypothesis and say "the most incomprehensible thing about the universe is that it's comprehensible."

Another element that seems impossible to ignore is DNA. DNA is in every cell, is its own language, and the mechanism by which all life has the ability to recreate itself. Life advances constantly and DNA has the blueprint. The DNA in a single strand, stretched out, would be over 6 ft long. In that single strand, you would have more information than all 30 volumes of the encyclopedia Britannica. If you stretched out all the DNA in your body, it would go from Earth all the way to the Sun and back 61 times! All of this speaks to a Creator not random mutations over allegedly billions of years.

James Watson is given credit as the founder of what we now recognize as the double helix DNA strand. He suggested that something outside of our existence had to have put us here. Well doesn't that describe God? It's what the Bible tells us that "something" is, that God created all things.

Genesis 1, 1-4

1 In the beginning God created the heavens and the earth. 2 Now the earth was formless and empty, darkness was over the surface of the deep, and the Spirit of God was hovering over the waters. 3 And God said, "Let there be light," and there was light. 4 God saw that the light was good, and he separated the light from the darkness.

I would like to point out that on the PANDO app or to those of you who have internet capability, go to verse by verse ministry. You will see a creation study in which Albert Einstein's theory of relativity fits perfectly into the Genesis formula, it's incredible!

I would also like to point out how fragile, precise, and fine tuned our existence on earth is. According to current scientific understanding, there are around 26 fundamental constants that are considered necessary to sustain life on Earth. These constants represent the values of various forces and particles in the universe, all of which need to be precisely tuned for life to exist as we know it. I'm going to keep this as simple as possible.

The earth is 93 million miles away from the sun. Its proximity is perfect to sustain life on earth. Complete annihilation would occur if we were closer or further away. That's just the distance, take the elliptical orbit into consideration as well, all points to intelligent design.

Secondly, Gravity is crucial for sustaining life on Earth because it holds the planet's atmosphere in place, allowing us to breathe by trapping essential gases like oxygen, and it also plays a vital role in the development and function of all living organisms by influencing their structure and physiology, essentially sustaining life on Earth; without gravity, the atmosphere would dissipate into space, making life as we know it impossible.

Third, earth's elements, particularly carbon, hydrogen, oxygen, nitrogen, phosphorus, and sulfur, are crucial for sustaining life on the planet because they act as the building blocks for all living organisms, forming complex molecules like proteins, nucleic acids, and lipids necessary for cellular function and biological processes.

Dr. Francis Collins, Director of the National Human Genome Research Institute, studied quantum mechanics at Yale. He eventually went into medicine and was an atheist but never tested the evidence there might be a God. He eventually said by pure intellect it can bring you right up to the precipice of belief but then you must choose the next step. He eventually gave himself to Christ and acknowledged that given all the evidence and information available it would take far more faith to believe in the absence of God, than to accept that there is a divine creator.

I was surprised to learn that modern science was started by Christians. Galileo, Kepler, Boyle, and Newton are all names we are all familiar with. Many of the best scientists today are people of faith. Between 1901-2000 60% of Nobel Laureates were Christians. C.S. Lewis is quoted "men became scientists because they expected law in nature and they expected law in nature because they believed in a legislature." Isaac Newton's quote "This most beautiful system of the sun, planets, and comets could only proceed from the council and dominion of an intelligent and powerful being." I think it's fair to acknowledge science can't explain everything. Science explains the laws of nature but not where it came from. It can't explain how life began, can't explain purpose, or what it means to love.

I believe we can stand firm that we don't have a blind faith but a reasonable faith.

However, all this being said, I will take my own personal interactions and experiences to validate the existence of God. My whole purpose in writing this book has been the revelation of God throughout my life and to show the incredibly relational nature God wants with me and with you. This whole book has been a testimony of what God can do if we'll just put our hand in His. In fact, the more broken you think you are, the more likely it is you're a prime candidate to show God's glory.

Chapter 11

THE BIBLE

CAME TO BELIEVE (PART 2)

As I continued sitting in jail through much of 2024, this was the beginning of deconstructing what had been years of cynicism, and skepticism regarding the authenticity of the Bible. I remember being completely captivated by Dan Brown's book The Da Vinci Code, when it first came out in 2003. To someone who had already been skeptical of the bible, The Da Vinci Code gave a very tasty story of biblical scandal, and went as far as claiming Mary Magdalene and Jesus were married and had a child. Other claims were made for example that Jesus's divinity narrowly won on a close vote at the Council of Nicea, which ultimately determined the ruling on Jesus's divinity as the Christian religion claims. Turns out that "close vote" as the book suggested was actually 314-2!!

Something I need to interject here is what's referred to as confirmation bias. The encyclopedia Britannica's definition of confirmation bias is: the tendency to process information by looking for, or interpreting, information that is consistent with one's own existing beliefs. Prior to The Da Vinci Code in 2003, I had been fascinated by documentaries on the "Lost years of Jesus", The Gnostic Gospels, and esoteric meanings of what Jesus allegedly really meant through his teachings. There seemed to be compelling arguments made by scholars that naturally led me down the path that the Bible and its historical accuracy in any capacity was flawed.

I'll never forget one of the catchy pieces of debate that I heard regarding the Divinity of Jesus. It was stated that there was a significant question at the time whether Jesus was God who became a man, or was he a man who became one with God? The back half of that question completely eliminates Jesus's divinity and allows for there to be a pathway to cultivating the "I AM", spoken about in many other self-help, self deification books. It allows a pathway that somehow through higher States of consciousness we reach enlightenment, no need for a savior, we are our own God. Furthermore, it seems to be a condescending jab back at the Christian religion using Jesus as a way to debunk its own beliefs.

When I was originally incarcerated in 2008, I had begun reading other books and materials that I have previously mentioned. What I had done was put myself in an echo chamber of material confirming what I thought I already knew. I wasn't getting any information relative to the other side of the Bible's authenticity as seen through the lenses of biblical scholars. I have always enjoyed processing life through my logic and these arguments about the most important topic relative to the eternity of my soul appeared to make sense. Jesus was a prophet of sorts, certainly an enlightened being, but not God incarnated as a human.

So as my revisiting of the Christian theology now in 2024 continued, I want to make it clear this had been my belief system. However, I realized in order to be receptive to new information I couldn't come to God with a full cup. It seemed pretty obvious I was being tapped on my spiritual shoulder by God given what I have shared with you in this book. I needed only to be open-minded and willing.

I could feel God as I continued to ask in prayer, "What do you want from me?" I would like to mention the title for this book, and all of the chapter titles were revealed to me as I continued to watch The Chosen. I was captivated by the show's ability to demonstrate the biblical narrative so closely and personalize Jesus. I felt like I was developing a relationship with Jesus more and more with each episode. The other consistent answer to my prayer was God instructing me to go to drug rehab. As I listened to more and more sermons and read my Bible. There was a very clear personal connection that I had never experienced before with God, and Jesus was becoming the glue. I was to continue asking my questions and eventually write this book.

Still, being a person of logic and liking to be able to back up why I believe what I believe, my journey continued. I've mentioned I have OCD and yet again God has met me and communicated in a language and manner that I'll understand- numbers. What I found out after researching the Bible for myself was going to simultaneously convince me of it's authenticity, and the divinity of Jesus

The Bible is truly like no other book. It's actually 66 different books separated by an Old Testament (39 books) and New Testament (27 books). 400 years separate the Old and New Testament. It's written over the span of 1500 years, by 40 different authors, on 3 different continents, in 3 different languages by kings, peasants, fisherman, doctors and scribes.

2 Timothy 3:16 says, All Scripture is God-breathed and is useful for teaching, rebuking, correcting, and training in righteousness.

Looking at the concept of creation as a whole, if there was a creator, there would be a couple of ways God could communicate with that creation. One of those would be by leaving a divine fingerprint. I've made my case for that in the Proof of God segment. Another way would be to communicate directly with the creation, in this case, a written word. Within that written word because the divine Creator is outside the realm of time, prophecy would be very relevant to those God is attempting to communicate with. In other words, documentation of what is to come.

There are over 300 prophecies in the Old Testament describing details of the coming messiah, his lineage, death, and future events. I am going to just point out 8:

1. He would be born of a virgin (Isaiah 7:14)

2. The Messiah would be born in the town of Bethlehem (Micah 5:2) (population was less than 1000 at time of Jesus' birth)

3. The Messiah would have a forerunner (John the Baptist) (Isaiah 40:3-5)

4. The Messiah would be rejected and betrayed by a friend (Psalms 55:12-14)

5. The betrayal would be for 30 pieces of silver (Zechariah 11:12–13)

6. He would be mocked and spit on and they would cast lots for his clothing (Psalm 22:18)

7. His bones wouldn't be broken in death (Psalm 34:20)

8. His hands and feet would be pierced (Psalm 22:16) (crucifixion wasn't even invented for 800 more years!)

Mathematician Peter Stoner and 600 of his students counted the probability of a single man fulfilling just 8 of the Old Testament prophecies. That number would be an incomprehensible 1 in 100,000,000,000,000,000 quadrillion. He later indicated that Jesus fulfilled more than 324 prophecies which puts the probabilities at 1 to the 10th power followed by 157 zeros after it!!!

Professor Stoner illustrated this probability in a more visual manner. He stated that if 100 quadrillion silver dollars were laid down within the geographic boundaries of the state of Texas, they would cover every square inch of the state and would amass a pile two feet high across the state.

With only one of these silver dollars marked with an X on it; a man would be blindfolded, placed in the middle of the state and told to walk in any direction for as far as he wishes, the probability as calculated is expressed as that man selecting the one and only silver dollar with a X marking on it!

Once the overall probability calculation was completed and reviewed by Professor Stoner, the work was submitted for review by the American Scientific Affiliation and their findings are stated as follows:

The work has been reviewed by members of the American Scientific Affiliation and its Executive Council and has been found, in general, to be dependable and accurate in regard to the scientific material presented. The mathematical analysis included is based upon principles of probability which are thoroughly sound, and Professor Stoner has applied these principles in a proper and convincing way.

Some critics argue that the interpretation of these prophecies can be subjective, with some passages being applied to Jesus after the fact, which can skew the statistical analysis. This kind of skepticism I felt to have been a fair and objective point that warranted further inquiry. Additionally, is it possible that the Old Testament documents were changed at some point in an attempt to validate the popularity of Christianity? If this last hurdle could be overcome, I knew I would be convinced.

In 1947 in Qumran, a young boy stumbled across the greatest archaeological Discovery in the history of mankind, what we now call the Dead Sea Scrolls. Over the next 10 years, 800 scrolls would be found in 11 different caves. Every book of the Old Testament with the exception of Esther, was perfectly preserved by the arid climate for over 2,000 years! When the scrolls were analyzed the only differences between the Old Testament you have in your Bible now, were found to be grammatical errors. For example an extra "n" put on the name John, nothing to change its content or meaning.. not only did it validate the historical accuracy of the bible, it nullified any transcription errors that are alleged because there are copies of copies of the Bible. This verified the authenticity of the Bible as well as validated Jesus's divinity at the same time. There is one cohesive message throughout a 1500 year narrative. The bible has no contradictions and to date there hasn't been 1 archaeological find to nullify its authenticity.

To close out this section I'd like to point out another staggering piece of the Bible's literary dominance compared to other ancient texts. The New Testament was written between 50-100 AD. The earliest copy was found in 130 AD, which is less than 100 years from the original to the first copy being found. There were 5,600 copies, with a staggering 99.5% accuracy. To put that in perspective, writings from Plato, Caesar, and Socrates aren't even in the ballpark. The closest is Homer's Iliad. Written in 900 BC with the first copy found in 400 BC. That puts it at 500 years between the original and the first copy found. There were 643 copies of Homer's Iliad found, again compared to 5600 copies of the New Testament. If you add in the old testament, there are over 24,000 copies of the Bible from ancient times. When it comes to the historical accuracy of ancient texts, the Bible has no competition.

Below is a chart showing the comparisons of ancient literary documents and how they compare to the Bible.

ANCIENT MANUSCRIPT COMPARISON CHART

Author	Date Written	Earliest Copy	Approximate Time Span between original & copy	# of Copies	Accuracy of Copies
Lucretius	died 55 or 53 B.C.		1100 yrs	2	---
Pliny	A.D. 61-113	A.D. 850	750 yrs	7	---
Plato	427-347 B.C.	A.D. 900	1200 yrs	7	---
Demosthenes	4th Cent. B.C.	A.D. 1100	800 yrs	8	---
Herodotus	480-425 B.C.	A.D. 900	1300 yrs	8	---
Suetonius	A.D. 75-160	A.D. 950	800 yrs	8	---
Thucydides	460-400 B.C.	A.D. 900	1300 yrs	8	---
Euripides	480-406 B.C.	A.D. 1100	1300 yrs	9	---
Aristophanes	450-385 B.C.	A.D. 900	1200	10	---
Caesar	100-44 B.C.	A.D. 900	1000	10	---
Livy	59 BC-AD 17	---	???	20	---
Tacitus	circa A.D. 100	A.D. 1100	1000 yrs	20	---
Aristotle	384-322 B.C.	A.D. 1100	1400	49	---
Sophocles	496-406 B.C.	A.D. 1000	1400 yrs	193	---
Homer (Iliad)	900 B.C.	400 B.C.	500 yrs	643	95%
New Testament	1st Cent. A.D. (A.D. 50-100)	2nd Cent. A.D. (c. A.D. 130 f.)	less than 100 years	5600	99.5%

NOTES:
- There are thousands more New Testament Greek manuscripts than any other ancient writing.

Chapter 12

The Resurrection

Came To Believe (Part 3)

I'm going to begin this section with the presupposition that the existence of Jesus of Nazareth is a fact. It shocked me to find people will go to any length in an attempt to defend their beliefs and in some cases this included denying the existence of Jesus. There are numerous recordings of Jesus outside the Bible and the death of Jesus is acknowledged as historical fact documented by Josephus, Tacitus, and Lucian all of which were the ruling authorities of that era.

After I came to believe in the Bible's authenticity and Jesus' divinity, the resurrection still loomed as a tough sell. Is it possible Jesus really died and rose 3 days later? I felt comfortable in the Bible's authenticity, but was going to need help in verifying this alleged incident over 2,000 years ago.. If Christ wasn't resurrected there is no Christian religion. Paul, who authored nearly 70% of the New Testament, makes the following bold assertion.

1 Corinthians 15:3-8

Christ died for our sins according to the Scriptures, that he was buried, that he was raised on the third day according to the Scriptures, and that he appeared to Cephas, and then to the Twelve. After that, he appeared to more than five hundred of the brothers and sisters at the same time, most of whom are still living, though some have fallen asleep (died). Then he appeared to James (Jesus' half-brother) then to all the apostles, last of all me.

Paul doubles down on the significance and importance of the Resurrection in the following statement:

1 Corinthians 15:13-17

If there is no resurrection of the dead, then not even Christ has been raised. And if Christ has not been raised, our preaching is useless and so is your faith. More than that, we are then found to be false witnesses about God, for we have testified about God that he raised Christ from the dead. But he did not raise him if in fact the dead are not raised. For if the dead are not raised, then Christ has not been raised either. And if Christ has not been raised, your faith is futile; you are still in your sins.

Clearly, this is the foundational cornerstone to the entire Christian religion. I will share with you what my skepticisms, questions, and doubts were as I tackled this most improbable event. Although, considering I had personally been brought back from death, I must admit there's room for possibility. There were two big differences from my situation not to mention the implications. First the way in which Jesus died, and secondly, the length of time he was dead before being brought back.

The first question I had to ask was, did Jesus actually die on the cross? If somehow Jesus had not died on the cross, certainly it could explain why so many people claimed to have seen him after his alleged death. I remember reading a book when I was in prison that presented the hypothesis that perhaps Jesus never died on the cross? This hypothesis however has no merit, let me explain. Jesus was sentenced by Pontius Pilate to be scourged (flogged), and then crucified, guilty of alleged blasphemy. The usual instrument used for a flogging was a short whip with several single or braided leather thongs of variable lengths, in which small iron balls or sharp pieces of sheep bones were tied at intervals. Jesus was stripped of his clothing, and his hands were tied to an upright post. These straps are then flung like a whip against the body. As the flogging continued, the lacerations would tear into the underlying skeletal muscles and produce quivering ribbons of bleeding flesh. It was brutal and brought Jesus to the precipice of death, but meant to keep him alive just long enough to be crucified.

The crucifixion itself involves large spikes driven through the wrist area as well as the feet to a wooden cross and then elevated. Due to the positioning of the body, inhalation becomes nearly impossible. Adequate exhalation required lifting the body by pushing up on the feet and by flexing the elbows and pulling the shoulders inward. The two most prominent causes of death to Jesus were shock from inadequate blood flow to critical organs due to blood loss. And secondly inadequate oxygen levels in the blood due to the inability to breathe properly. Death by crucifixion was, in every sense of the word, excruciating (Latin, excruciatus, or "out of the cross")

The following is a quote from the Gospel of John

So that the bodies might not remain on the cross on the Sabbath, because it was a preparation day (for that Sabbath was a high day), requested of Pilate that their legs might be broken and the bodies be taken away. Then the soldiers came and broke the legs of the first one, and the legs of the other who was crucified with Jesus. But when they came to Jesus and saw that He was already dead, they did not break His legs; (His bones wouldn't be broken in death Psalm 34:20) but one of the soldiers had pierced His side with a spear, and immediately blood and water had come out" (John 19:30-34).

Clearly, the weight of historical and medical evidence indicates that Jesus was dead before the wound to his side was inflicted and supports the traditional view that the spear, thrust between his right ribs, probably perforated not only the right lung but also his heart and thereby ensured his death. Since no one was intended to survive crucifixion, the body was not released to the family until the soldiers were sure that the victim was dead. No one was ever documented to have survived a Roman crucifixion. The Romans had perfected the art of what is considered the most torturous and prolonged way to die. I hope I have made my case, Jesus most certainly had died.

Keep in mind Jesus was crucified on a Friday, so removing him from the cross was necessary to do before sundown as the Sabbath was approaching. This was the other reason they were breaking the legs of those crucified with Jesus so the proper burial procedures according to Jewish law could be met in a timely manner. It should be noted that Joseph of Arimathea personally went to Pontius Pilate and asked if he could have the body of Jesus and bury it in a tomb that belonged to him. After his crucifixion, Jesus' body was taken down from the cross and anointed with myrrh, aloes, ointments and other spices before he was buried (Luke 23:56; John 19:39-40).

As sundown was approaching, there was speculation Jesus's disciples or followers may attempt to steal the body from the tomb.

In Matthew 27:62-66, the chief priests and Pharisees, fearing that Jesus's disciples might steal the body and claim he had risen, asked Pilate to have the tomb guarded.

As a result, two Roman soldiers were sent to guard the tomb and a 2-ton circular stone was rolled in front of it. A Roman seal was then placed above the tomb essentially claiming dominion over the area. Prior to Jesus's crucifixion, the disciples were filled with fear and grief and went into hiding. They sought refuge in a locked room in Jerusalem, likely in an upper room. They remained there for days concerned that they too would be subjugated to punishment if found. Just to reset, Jesus is dead, buried in a tomb, guarded by 2 Roman soldiers, secured with a 2 ton Stone represented with the Roman seal, and all of the disciples in hiding.

The best perspective on what convinced me of the resurrection came from pastor Chad Moore at Sun Valley Church in Arizona. Much of what I am about to share are notes that I took while in jail off of the PANDO app listening to pastor Chad. I was then able to follow up and do my own research once I got to rehab. As stated before, science is a tool in the toolbox but cannot prove everything. To those that would say you cannot scientifically prove the resurrection, you are absolutely right. You cannot scientifically prove that Jesus existed or that Abraham Lincoln was the 16th president. There are many things that we believe and accept outside the realm of science.

Encyclopedia Britannica defines scientific proof as follows: scientific proof is based on showing something is a fact based on repeating the event. It is done in a controlled environment where observations can be made, data drawn, and empirically verified. Given this definition, nothing in history could ever be proven by science.

There is also what is referred to as legal historical proof. It is based on something being a fact beyond a reasonable doubt. We reach a verdict on the weight of the evidence and have no rational basis for denying the decision. It depends on three kinds of testimony, oral, written, and exhibit (artifact). What follows is chapter 20 in The Gospel of John as to what happens next:

From the book of John
20 Early on the first day of the week, while it was still dark, Mary Magdalene went to the tomb and saw that the stone had been removed from the entrance. 2 So she came running to Simon Peter and the other disciple, the one Jesus loved, and said, "They have taken the Lord out of the tomb, and we don't know where they have put him!" 3 So Peter and the other disciple started for the tomb. 4 Both were running, but the other disciple outran Peter and reached the tomb first. 5 He bent over and looked in at the strips of linen lying there but did not go in. 6 Then Simon Peter came along behind him and went straight into the tomb. He saw the strips of linen lying there, 7 as well as the cloth that had been wrapped around Jesus' head. The cloth was still lying in its place, separate from the linen. 8 Finally the other disciple, who had reached the tomb first, also went inside. He saw and believed. 9 (They still did not understand from Scripture that Jesus had to rise from the dead.) 10 Then the disciples went back to where they were staying.

11 Now Mary stood outside the tomb crying. As she wept, she bent over to look into the tomb 12 and saw two angels in white, seated where Jesus' body had been, one at the head and the other at the foot. 13 They asked her, "Woman, why are you crying?" "They have taken my Lord away," she said, "and I don't know where they have put him." 14 At this, she turned around and saw Jesus standing there, but she did not realize that it was Jesus. He asked her, "Woman, why are you crying? Who is it you are looking for?" Thinking he was the gardener, she said, "Sir, if you have carried him away, tell me where you have put him, and I will get him." Jesus said to her, "Mary."

She turned toward him and cried out in Aramaic, "Rabboni!" (which means "Teacher").
Jesus said, "Do not hold on to me, for I have not yet ascended to the Father. Go instead to my brothers and tell them, 'I am ascending to my Father and your Father, to my God and your God.'" Mary Magdalene went to the disciples with the news: "I have seen the Lord!" And she told them that he had said these things to her.

I've inserted the entire sequence according to the Gospel Of John to make the beginning of multiple significant points that validated the resurrection in my mind.

1. Jesus appeared to Mary Magdalene first. If you were going to attempt to make an assertion of this magnitude, which became the launching point of the largest religion in the world, you wouldn't have started it with a woman. Why? Women during the time of Jesus weren't even deemed credible witnesses! They would have used a man or someone of solidified status to have made such an incredible statement.

2. The Roman guards we're gone. Something obviously frightened them and they fled.

3. A broken Roman Seal-the seal represented the authority of the emperor of Rome. These were trained men to guard it with their life. If they failed they would be crucified upside down.

4. A 2-ton Stone had been moved away. Who would have done this? The soldiers? Obviously not. The disciples? They were hiding for fear of their own lives.

5. Jesus was buried very close to where he had been crucified, so his body would have been in the immediate area. The story of the empty tomb was preached in Jerusalem to people who

had just watched Jesus die. The story of his resurrection wouldn't have survived one day because all they would have had to do was simply produce Jesus's body. Look at how far this actually went:

Matthew 28:12-15 Then the priests met with the elders and made a plan. They paid soldiers a large amount of money and said to them, "Tell the people that Jesus' followers came during the night and stole the body while you were asleep."

They themselves are acknowledging Jesus's body is gone! So it seems quite clear the body of Jesus is not where it had been laid to rest.

6. The witnesses. I'm going to discuss Paul in further detail in a little while, but I would like to again mention the previous scripture from Corinthians written by Paul.

He appeared to Cephas, and then to the Twelve. After that, he appeared to more than five hundred of the brothers and sisters at the same time, most of whom are still living, though some have fallen asleep (died). Then he appeared to James (Jesus' half-brother) then to all the apostles, last of all me.

7. The impact of Jesus. Jesus only had a 3-year ministry, never wrote a book, all of time is based off of his life. Your birthday and mine is acknowledged based on the existence of Jesus Christ. We acknowledge time in history according to: BC(before Christ) and AD(Anno Domini).

8. What convinced me however, is that all of the disciples died a martyr's death. The disciples went on to preach about the gospel, and that they had seen the resurrected Jesus. It's quite obvious that throughout history for numerous different reasons, people have died for what they believe to be true.

People have also died for what turned out to be a lie. BUT PEOPLE DON'T DIE FOR LIES THEY KNOW TO BE LIES! THE DISCIPLES KNEW!!! All of them were killed with the exception of John, as a result of preaching Jesus's teachings and not recanting their statement that they had seen the resurrected Jesus. Below is a list of the disciples and how they died. These men died not for their belief, but because of what they saw.

Peter-crucified upside down
Andrew - crucified
James son of Zebedee - sword
John son of Zebedee - natural causes
Philip - crucified
Bartholomew (Nathaniel)- crucified
Thomas - spear
Matthew - sword
James - crucified
Thaddeus - arrows
Simon the zealot - crucified
Judas- hung himself

Another point of interest is Initially, James, the half-brother of Jesus, was a skeptic who didn't believe Jesus was the Messiah. After all, he had grown up with Jesus his whole life. Could you imagine your half brother telling you that he was God! However after Jesus' resurrection, he became a devout believer and a leader in the early church and also died because of his faith.

The significance of Paul really warrants its own chapter. Paul was formerly known by the name Saul. He was a Pharisee and one of if not the main enemy of Jesus's followers prior to his conversion. In the book of Acts He does not see Jesus as Lord, and strives to persecute the fledgling church. While on the road to Damascus to confront the Christians there, Paul is overcome by a flash of heavenly light. He hears the voice of the Lord crying out to him – "Saul, why do you persecute me?" Paul is blinded by this encounter with Jesus, and he is led by hand to Damascus where Christ instructs him to wait. Paul prays and fasts for three days. On the third day, Jesus appears to Ananias — one of the disciples Paul was coming to persecute — and sends him to greet Paul. Ananias, while initially fearful, finds the blinded Paul and greets him as a brother. Ananias lays his hands on Paul, and the apostle's sight is restored as something like scales fall from his eyes. Paul is immediately baptized, and the church's great enemy becomes her great advocate.

We know Paul's conversion is roughly 3 years after Jesus's crucifixion. As a result Paul went to visit James (Jesus' now converted half-brother), and Peter to discuss and investigate what they had seen regarding the resurrection. What was revealed to Paul during that visit I'd like to quote Dr James Dunn, "this tradition we can be entirely confident it was created as a Creed as tradition within months of the death of Jesus."

I have shared with you over the last three chapters how and why I came to believe. With the exception of the prophetic, statistical slam dunk that Jesus had to be the Messiah, I look at the preponderance of the evidence as if everything else is a circumstantial evidence case. I can't tell you how many guys I did time with that just ONE witness convicted them and sent them to prison. In the case of the resurrection, Jesus appeared to 500 people at one time. Paul even says, "most of whom are still living, but some have fallen asleep", he's encouraging and challenging people to go ask for themselves. Given the totality of the evidence, I feel very confident in my belief.

One last point I'd like to bring up, because as I've continued to do my own investigating the mass sightings of Jesus after the resurrection has some skeptics. There have been claims because of guilt, or what would have been diagnosed as PTSD at the time, were these mass "sightings" hallucinations? I even heard one person say "well there's sightings of Bigfoot." To address the last statement first, that's what's referred to as a categorical error. Simply put, those are mostly all individual sightings. We have over 500 witnesses, not 1. So the comparison of one person claiming to have seen Bigfoot versus hundreds of people having seen the risen Christ, it's not an applicable argument. Additionally, modern-day psychologists will tell you hallucinations occur in individuals, not groups of people. Again with this many people as witnesses, including those that were willing to be put to death for what they knew they had seen, I'm comfortable in my position of belief. Not to mention the doubters still can't produce the body- everyone at the time knew Jesus wasn't in the tomb.

Chapter 13

DO YOU WANT TO BE HEALED?

As I begin to close out this book, I would like to bring up The Chosen again because one of my favorite scenes opened my eyes to my own healing process. The story takes place at the Pool of Bethesda in Jerusalem. It's a place where people with various ailments would gather, believing that an angel would stir the water at certain times, and the first person to enter would be healed. A man who had been sick and paralyzed for 38 years was lying by the pool, unable to enter the water himself. Jesus walks by, sees the man and asks him:

"DO YOU WANT TO BE HEALED?"

The man explains that he has no one to help him into the pool when the water is stirred, and by the time he gets to the pool, someone else is always there first. Jesus tells the man to "get up, pick up your mat, and walk," and immediately the man is healed and able to do so.

Everytime I watch the scene, I get tears in my eyes. I find myself in so many ways relating to the paralytic, not in a physical way, but behaviorally. I've given every excuse and coupon, real or perceived, not to recover. I have been giving away my identity as a child of God and allowing a false narrative to live in my head rent free. During the process of writing this book, I have been chasing freedom and finding God, just as hard as I chased dope, and I have found many answers.

Do You Want to be healed?

Life isn't linear is it? How is it that in less than 24 hours it can seem as if all your best efforts, intentions, and hard work seem to have gotten you nowhere? At times it feels as if life has catapulted me into the deepest darkest hole of despair and depression and at other times, it seems like a magical, mystical, joyride in which everyone seems to be smiling?

Do you want to be healed?

I suppose this is the ebb and flow of being human and enjoying its ups and downs. However, it has been revealed to me that as human beings we are composed of mind, body, spirit, and emotion. If God continues to grant me the gifts of experiencing his creation, it seems only fair that I attempt to integrate these aspects of my nature. When life seems out of whack, sometimes I just try to stay in the moment and allow myself to feel whatever it is that I'm experiencing.

Do you want to be healed?

It also reminds me of the acronym HALT:

Hungry
Angry
Lonely
Tired

If I am utilizing the gift of awareness that God has given me, I can usually find a bad mood, energy, attitude, or any other typical place of discomfort, and remind myself to look in these four categories and see if any of them need addressing and if so, to do so.

Do you want to be healed?

At times, it pisses me off that I may have that level of control of my life as I prefer to point outward and make it someone else's fault for my emotional or attitudinal problem.

That reminds me of the following prayer many of you know:

God, grant me the serenity to accept the things I cannot change, courage to change the things I can, and the wisdom to know the difference.

Do you want to be healed?

While that prayer is phenomenal and has helped millions of people I want to point something out to you that was pointed out to me- watch what happens when you add the letter s to the word grant in the prayer:

God GRANTS me the serenity to accept the things I cannot change, courage to change the things I can, and the wisdom to know the difference.

To me, this takes it from a position of me asking God, to me claiming what God has already done for me and will continue to do. All that needs to be done is for me to put my hand on his. It requires me to show up in my own life, as God loves you and I so much, he will never force himself upon us but will always be there when we are ready. If God seems far away, who moved?

Do You Want to be Healed?

How do I sustain my freedom? Two things come to mind? First, I remember a quote from the Big Book of Alcoholics Anonymous, " What we have is a daily reprieve based upon the maintenance of our spiritual condition." Every day I go to God, ask for strength, guidance, and direction. I remember that by serving others I serve myself.

Do you want to be healed?

Secondly, I stay committed to my purpose. And I stay committed to my purpose by being connected to the vine.

John 15:1-5

"I am the true vine, and my Father is the gardener. 2 He cuts off every branch in me that bears no fruit, while every branch that does bear fruit he prunes[a] so that it will be even more fruitful. 3 You are already clean because of the word I have spoken to you. 4 Remain in me, as I also remain in you. No branch can bear fruit by itself; it must remain in the vine. Neither can you bear fruit unless you remain in me.

5 "I am the vine; you are the branches. If you remain in me and I in you, you will bear much fruit; apart from me you can do nothing. 6 If you do not remain in me, you are like a branch that is thrown away and withers; such branches are picked up, thrown into the fire and burned.

Do You Want to be Healed?

My father said to me "son, you haven't learned how to handle your freedom", he was absolutely right. Freedom, without purpose, is suicide for an addict. My purpose, in part, has been to share my journey with all of you and write this book to show you how God has been interacting with me all my life. Writing this book has been an incredible experience that no words can capture or articulate. My whole life has been an apprenticeship for where I am today, so has yours. One of my goals as I started this book was to be as transparent and honest as I could, so that you and I could identify with one another, and heal. But what would a life of being healed look like?

Do You Want to be Healed?

Healing, it can be scary. It can be wonderful. It can be exciting. And, it can be terrifying! You're going somewhere you've never been before. You're becoming a version of yourself that never existed. That is why we resist change and growth so often. It's stepping into the unknown. It's trusting that there is something vital on the other side. It is an act of Faith to continue to heal, change, and progress. You are boldly going in the chapters of a book you have never read yet. You are writing your story as you go, and there is no control. No predictability. No safety net. No comfort zone. As we heal, we leap forward trusting the next step will appear. So yeah, if healing and change make you afraid, that just means you're doing it right. You are in the darkness between where you were and where you are going. Trust it. Stumble forward. Enjoy the climb to the top of YOUR mountain. And enjoy the view! Be Still and Know That I Am God!

Do you want to be healed?

Trust in God
Believe in yourself
Dare to dream

CONCLUSION

Although I have come to believe in the Christian theology, I haven't miraculously been cured of my humanness. As someone who has identified as an addict most of my life, there are still times I think about getting high. When I first realized I had a problem with drugs, it was shown to me there were far deeper issues that were the cause, getting high was a symptom, an effect. No doubt I've had to work through many issues while in rehab, but at the end of the day, this simply comes down to a choice of what I want more.

Matthew 6:24 says, No one can serve two masters, for either he will hate the one and love the other, or he will be devoted to the one and despise the other.

The heavy metal band Metallica is by far my favorite group. Their music and lyrics are on another level compared to any other band in my generation. Metallica's "Master of Puppets" album was inducted into the Library of Congress's National Recording Registry in 2015, becoming the first metal album to be recognized for its cultural, historical, and aesthetic significance. The song Master of Puppets is the perfect lyrical description of an addict obeying it's Master- drugs. I can personally testify, I would not have lived some days had I not had access to listening to this song. It's time to choose which "Master" I will serve.

In the same way we wouldn't try to build a house without first having a blueprint, it's important for me to remember I am the product of a creator. Doesn't it make sense that if I'm a product of a creator that I would want to know how I was created and what my relationship is with that creator? I cannot explain in my finite human mind, the infinite mind of that which created me. I think God welcomes our questions, doubts, and can handle our anger, even when it's at Him. It's reasonable to doubt God. Look at the examples of how God responds in the Bible when doubts and anger arose:

1. Peter, while standing on the water, takes his eyes off Jesus and begins to sink. Does Jesus let him drown, upset with Peter? Of course not, Jesus replies,"Why did you doubt?" It wasn't meant to be accusatory, but the rhetorical question of a loving father who then reaches down to pick up one of his children. Wouldn't any of us do the same?

2. When Jesus arrived in Bethany, Martha, Lazarus's sister, met him, expressing her grief and acknowledging that if Jesus had been there earlier, her brother would not have died. Jesus responded to Martha's words with a promise and a declaration of his identity: "Your brother will rise again". He then went on to say, "I am the resurrection and the life. Whoever believes in me, though he may die, he shall live, and whoever lives and believes in me shall never die". The response from Jesus was one of assurance and affirmation, not rejection.

3. Thomas after the resurrection: Jesus responded to Thomas's doubts by inviting him to touch his wounds, saying, "Put your finger here, and see my hands; and put out your hand, and place it in my side. Do not disbelieve, but believe," before stating, "Have you believed because you have seen me? Blessed are those who have not seen and yet have believed". No condescension, no scolding, no I told you so, but a loving compassionate response of reassurance.

I've been the most selfish person I've ever known and no one ever mattered enough to keep me from doing what I wanted to do. Despite knowing the outcome from dozens and dozens of previous binges, I fed the beast at the cost of losing quality people, jobs, cars, and homes. The best "quality person" I lost though, was me. Through the restorative grace of Christ, today, I am proud of myself in a healthy way and I've done my best to share with you what my experience as a flawed human has looked like. God can take the worst situation and through you, with you, turn it around. However, I had to learn that I had to show up in my own life, I had to want to be healed. Many of my hardships in life have been self-created with irrational and immature responses. I have found peace as a result of acceptance. And that word acceptance for me means no longer having a negative reaction due to the pain of my own resistance.

We live in an "instant world." Instagram, instacart, fast food, a microwave society, dopamine overload with constant access to online gambling, Facebook reels, and YouTube shorts. We have lost our trust, and understanding of the value, worth and importance of processes. I need to slow life down and cultivate discipline.

I would like to acknowledge Dr. Anna Lembke's book Dopamine Nation again. In the conclusion of her book she summarizes 10 main takeaways on how to overcome addiction. One of which I would like to share here...

"Instead of running away from the world, we can find escape by immersing ourselves in it."

      Romans 12:2

Do not conform to the pattern of this world, but be transformed by the renewing of your mind.

We are living a conscious or an unconscious program all of our lives. Our subconscious mind controls 90 % of our brain. Nearly 65,000 thoughts go through our mind everyday, and 85% of those are negative. It takes conscious awareness to identify the thought, and through developing our emotional intelligence, not to attach to it.

I can't explain what happened to me when I died and heard "Do you want to go back?" There's an invisible world going on all around us. I now believe that consciousness and awareness aren't connected to the brain, but our spirit. Trying to find consciousness in the brain is like trying to find time in a clock. In the same way a clock measures time, our brain becomes a processor for the realm of consciousness, but our brain doesn't generate consciousness. While I can't prove it scientifically, I experienced it. We can't "see" gravity, but we can observe its effect. I'm at a point where all that matters is I've had an opportunity to share this incredible experience with you. It also led me on a journey to become closer to God. Doubt strengthened my faith, and through my doubts, I found my answers.

CONTACT INFORMATION

SAMUEL GEORGE
PHONE NUMBER 352-426-0723
EMAIL notallsnakesrattle@gmail.com
Facebook Not All Snakes Rattle
YouTube Not All Snakes Rattle

www.ingramcontent.com/pod-product-compliance
Lightning Source LLC
Chambersburg PA
CBHW060838050426
42453CB00008B/738